8 When It's Your Second Time Around   217

Staying Sane™

When You're Planning Your WEDDING

Staying Sane™
When You're
Planning Your
WEDDING

Pam Brodowsky
Evelyn Fazio

Da Capo
LIFE
LONG

A Member of the Perseus Books Group

Set in 11.5-point ITC New Baskerville by the Perseus Books Group

Library of Congress Cataloging-in-Publication Data
Brodowsky, Pamela K.
  Staying sane when you're planning your wedding / Pam Brodowsky,
Evelyn Fazio.—1st Da Capo Press ed.
      p.   cm.—(Staying sane)
  ISBN-13: 978-0-7382-1056-8 (pbk. : alk. paper)
  ISBN-10: 0-7382-1056-0 (pbk. : alk. paper)
  1. Weddings—Planning.   2. Wedding etiquette.   I. Fazio, Evelyn M.
II. Title.
  HQ745.B86 2007
  395.2'2—dc22

                                                                    2006035582

First Da Capo Press edition 2007

Published by Da Capo Press
A Member of the Perseus Books Group
www.dacapopress.com

Da Capo Press books are available at special discounts for bulk purchases in the U.S. by corporations, institutions, and other organizations. For more information, please contact the Special Markets Department at the Perseus Books Group, 11 Cambridge Center, Cambridge, MA 02142, or call (800) 255-1514 or (617) 252-5298, or e-mail special.markets@perseusbooks.com.

1 2 3 4 5 6 7 8 9

The authors would like
to dedicate this book to everyone
who is about to tie the knot,
who already has, and who will do so
some time in the future, especially our readers,
our friends, and our families.

Contents

1   When Time Is of the Essence   1

2

When You're Planning a Destination Wedding or an Unconventional Venue   31

3

When the Cultures Aren't Common   67

About the Staying Sane Series

The Staying Sane series is a collection of funny, irreverent, lighthearted, yet sassy, advice-laden books that are dedicated to finding the silver lining in the annoying, frustrating, or trying situations we all encounter every single day.

The Staying Sane series shows you how to look for, and find, the humor and enlightenment in nearly every situation—you only need to be open to seeing it. Let's face it: We all experience difficult or trying times in our lives, and that's precisely why we've developed the Staying Sane series.

We want you to know that we've been through all kinds of demented things ourselves (Oh, have we ever!), and we and our contributors plan to focus each volume on a specific topic to help you cope with some of the most trying, most typical—and least sane—situations all of us face at one point or another as we try to get through life.

Unlike any other books, the Staying Sane series' intention is to shed light on what can be difficult situations, to bring laughter to people who are caught up in a web of frustration and petty annoyances, and to provide help, advice, and answers—while letting readers know they are not the only ones who've suffered through these same irritating episodes or circumstances. Since laughter is truly the best medicine, the Staying Sane series will help you get through whatever comes up with as few bruises as possible, and, we hope, with your family relationships and friendships still intact when all is said (or not) and done (or not!).

If you're like us, just hearing about other people's problems usually makes our own seem trivial by comparison, making us realize that things aren't really so bad. What's more, by reading about the scores of other people who've had the same or worse experience, we are able to find a more realistic perspective and regain our sense of proportion—all because we've been able to step back and see that things really could be much worse. And besides, misery loves company!

Staying sane isn't as hard as you think. Keeping it together when all hell breaks loose is just part of life—something we have to do every single day if we're living on planet Earth. But keep one thing in mind: there is always someone else out there who is also on the edge of losing it. We all lead complicated lives, but this doesn't mean we can't laugh at our problems—it can really help make them seem smaller and less overwhelming.

So, when things seem to be getting out of hand and you just don't think you can take it anymore, pick up a copy of one of the Staying Sane titles. It may be just what you need to keep from going off the deep end. We'll be right there with you, helping you cope!

Let Us Know

We would be delighted to hear your reactions to the stories in this and all the other Staying Sane books. Please let us know which stories you liked best and how they related to your life.

We also would be very pleased if you'd send us your stories for upcoming volumes of the Staying Sane series. Is there a topic you'd like to see us cover? If so, let us know what it is you're looking for. We'll do our best to get a book into the works for you! Please write to us in care of our publisher.

We look forward to hearing from you!

Pam and Evelyn

About *Staying Sane When You're Planning Your Wedding*

Your wedding day is one of the most important days in your life, and it deserves to be celebrated with great joy and fanfare, in whatever way makes you happiest, whether it will be in a big church, on a beach in Hawaii, or in City Hall at lunchtime. However you decide to commemorate that special day, it will require planning. Now comes the tricky part.

Like most planned events, weddings involve countless details about wardrobe, food, and music; ceremonies, rituals, and rites. And all this requires you to make dozens—if not hundreds—of decisions. As if that's not enough to make your head spin, there's also the dreaded human factor: getting everyone to go along with what you want, with the least amount of commotion and fuss.

For example, what do you do if your bridesmaids don't get along? What if they all hate the dress you picked out? What if none of them looks good in the color you've chosen? How do you handle divorced parents who don't get along, the cousin who gets drunk at every wedding, and countless other details that are driving you crazy, taking the joy out of the moment, and dampening your enthusiasm for what should be one of the happiest experiences of your life?

Rather than let the snags undermine what should be such fun—planning your big event for the day your dreams come true—why not figure out a way to cope with it all? That's why we've created this book.

Each year, 2.3 million people get married, and each of them has to plan a wedding. All sorts of exciting and fun events surround these celebrations, but so do some unexpected and, shall we say, unplanned and maddening situations, reactions, behaviors, and annoyances—all seemingly destined to drive you crazy long before that special day ever arrives!

How do you handle it all? We've asked real people for their special stories about how they coped with every circumstance that popped up as they prepared for their big day. Here you'll find inspirational and funny tales of how others have dealt with many of the same—or, in some cases, even worse—situations that you're facing right at this very moment.

Sometimes just knowing you're not alone, and being able to find a bit of humor in what can be a trying time, may be just what you need to relax and enjoy the ride, instead of throwing in the towel and eloping to Vegas!

Staying Sane When You're Planning Your Wedding will help you find some levity in the planning process and all the related mishaps that go with it. Not only that, but it will provide tips and suggestions from the experts—those who've been through it already—to help lighten the load. Think of how much better you'll feel knowing you're not the only one who's suffered through the kind of stresses that can turn a fun, exciting time into a trial for everyone involved.

So, when things really seem to be getting out of hand, and you just don't think you can take it anymore, stop, take a deep breath, make yourself a cup of tea, sit down in a comfortable chair, kick off your shoes, and pick up your copy of *Staying Sane When You're Planning Your Wedding*. It may be just the thing you need to keep you from losing your mind. At the very least, for a few moments you'll have a break from thinking about whatever it was that was bothering you so much just now—and maybe you'll have a good laugh, too!

We all benefit from shared experience and can learn from what happened to someone else. We hope that you will be able to draw on the tips you've gained from the experts—our contributors—and handle things in a lighter, less stressful way. Just think of how much wear and tear you'll be saving everyone, especially yourself!

Congratulations on your upcoming marriage, and enjoy the ride!

1

When Time Is of the Essence

Sanity Quiz

You've been planning your wedding for almost nine months. It's now a week before your big day, and just when you thought you had everything worked out like clockwork, you realize you completely forgot about the band.

Do you
A. call the local talent agency and see what they can swing
B. ask all your friends if anybody can sing
C. call every DJ in the phone book
D. hire your cousin who plays spoons
E. reschedule the big day

However you answered this question, you'll want to know how our contributors saved the day when they had scheduling problems or last-minute changes. And hold on to your veil—they've been through it all!

Surviving Wedding Gown Shopping

Ronda Kaysen

IT LOOKED LIKE a pink-and-white silk escalator was crawling up my backside, halted only by a giant pink bow protruding from the small of my back.

"Beautiful!" gushed Olga, the fiftyish Russian sales-clerk with an enormous bosom and thick, fleshy hands. "This is the one!"

I would have turned around, but the train, which ended somewhere near my mother's feet at the other side of the room, was cumbersome. "I could drag the entire bridal party down the aisle on this thing," I said.

Olga was not amused. "Take it off! We try another!"

We were at the third bridal store of the day and my mother and sister, Gina, were looking a little weary.

Wedding gown shopping, I was discovering, was a far more exhausting experience than it appeared in the movies. The sample sizes fit no one, so each dress involved narrowing your eyes and trying to imagine what you might look like if the dress could actually fit over your thighs. And the salesclerks would sell you a burlap bag with a drawstring if you let them.

The next one, an antique beaded number, had a much more reasonable train. I spun around. "What do you think?"

My sister wrinkled her nose. "Kind of looks like a doily to me."

"Your breasts are swimming in it," my mother said.

"No problem!" rushed Olga. She stuffed two white nursing pads in my bra and readjusted my now conical boobs. "You see, you just need a little more padding."

"But it doesn't fit." My mother had taken to playing the bad cop for the day, grilling the saleswomen about delivery schedules and fabrics, doubting their promises of the wonders of tailoring. She walked over to me and grabbed hold of the extra fabric beneath my armpits.

"A tailor can fix that. No problem." Olga shooed my mom away and grabbed the fabric herself. "You just take it in here. Very simple." She stepped back to examine her creation. "You never know, she may get a little bit fat before the wedding."

The wedding dress shopping experience is adversarial. Salesclerks live on commission. Brides, faced with purchasing the single most expensive item of clothing they will ever own, are met with the reality that many wedding dresses are outrageously priced, cheap, tacky, and downright ugly. What many brides expect to be the fun part of the wedding experience is instead one fraught with fear of being cheated by the salesperson or, perhaps even worse, fear of walking down the aisle draped in a hideous frock.

A bride walks into a store thinking the clerk is trying to pull a fast one on her with unexpected costs like extra-length fees, complex alteration charges, and rush fees for dresses purchased within six months of the wedding date. Most samples come only in size 6 or 8 so the vast majority of brides cannot even fit into the dress they are expected to fall in love with and buy. Meanwhile, the clerk, who usually works on commission and by appointment only, is keenly aware that the bride at hand will likely buy nothing. And so exists a relationship built on mutual distrust.

The fellow brides I met standing in line at a Vera Wang sample sale were far better prepared than me. The woman behind me, a twenty-nine-year-old lawyer from Connecticut, clutched a giant binder filled with flyers, swatches, estimates, and illustrations. She pumped me for details about the few shops I had visited. When the extent of my inexperience became clear, she pummeled me with business cards and addresses of nearby bridal salons. The secret to finding the perfect dress, she said, was to avoid the showroom stores and stick to the boutiques. "You get more personal attention," she said, as we inched forward on the five-hour line with more than five hundred other brides-to-be.

After months of fruitless hunting, my wedding day was fast approaching and still I had seen nothing in my budget worth buying. My mother came to visit one bitter January weekend in an effort to finish my search.

First stop was a famous bridal store in Brooklyn that had recently moved to Manhattan. With sweeping white walls, a lofty waiting room, and a large showroom visible from the street, the store screamed "white wedding." It also charged you fifty dollars if you happened to cancel your appointment. Our salesclerk, a tiny middle-aged woman named Bonnie, greeted us with her assistant, a gaunt, humorless girl with bright red lipstick. Bonnie led us to a private changing room and asked us our budget. I said fifteen hundred dollars. She stared at me in horror. "There's very little in that range. Very little." She glared at my mother. "You can't get silk for less than fifteen hundred dollars."

"She tried on a silk gown in Sacramento that was a thousand," my mother shot back.

"It must have been a *blend*," Bonnie declared. "There's very little I can do for you."

Despite her dire predictions, Bonnie brought me a handful of dresses. "Take off your clothes," she ordered. I stripped down to my underwear and cowered in front of Bonnie and the red-lipped assistant. I felt foolish in my polka-dot panties. We made our way through several garish dresses until I settled on a strapless gown with a layered skirt. It was pretty enough. "It's silk *organza*," Bonnie drawled, drawing out "organza" with a long, nasally tone. She rubbed her hands over my thighs to demonstrate. "Stunning fabric. Just stunning."

"It's a little expensive," said my mom, "and it bunches at her crotch."

Bonnie ran her hands over my groin. "This dress is much too small. When she gets the right size it'll fall beautifully."

My mom squinted and puckered her lips. "The color isn't right."

Bonnie pulled out a packet of inch-long swatches. "Look at this one, the ivory. It's stunning."

I leaned over the swatch. My mother leaned over the swatch. We stared at it together. "I'm supposed to tell what the dress will look like from that?" my mom said.

"Follow me!" ordered Bonnie.

We traipsed into the main showroom to look at the swatch in better light. Bonnie held it up to the ceiling. She tilted it to the right. She tilted it to the left. She ran a finger along its edge. "Look at it. It's just stunning. Simply stunning."

"Stunning," whispered the red-lipped assistant.

Another bride-to-be stood on a pedestal, the skirt of her dress—a crinkled, curling, ever-expanding mass of tulle and silk and bows and beading—looked like a white bird's nest. "Isn't that dress just *gorgeous?*" gushed the assistant.

I smiled politely. Bonnie glared at her assistant. Clearly we were not to be distracted from the cause at hand: the blessed swatch.

"Well," said my mother, "we'll think about it and get back to you."

Bonnie staggered. She looked from me to my mother to her red-lipped assistant. I could see the cold chill of reality settling in: We were only browsing.

Bonnie shifted gears and moved in for the hard sell. "Get back to us? No. She has no time." She rapidly shook her head, her face reddening. "Her wedding is in *May!* There isn't time. She needs to order this week. No, today! She needs to order today. Or it can't possibly get here in time for the alterations."

Bonnie was coming unglued.

"Well, I need to think about it," I said.

"There isn't time to think. We're the biggest bridal showroom in the world. If we can't get you a dress before May no one can."

With that, Bonnie rushed off and returned with a lanky woman with measuring tape slung around her neck. This woman, apparently, was the tailor. The tailor concurred. I needed to order my dress at this very instant or risk the horror of what would come if I didn't.

My mother shrugged, "Well, I guess she'll have to get married naked."

With that, we extrapolated ourselves from Bonnie and her entourage, pushing back fears that I would, in fact, get married in the buff. How was it possible that four months was not enough time to buy a dress?

We ventured over to a private, appointment-only sample sale in the East Village. The dresses were tiny, dirty, and frayed. The only one that fit looked like it belonged on a middle-aged drag queen. "It's not the prettiest dress, but at eight hundred dollars you can't go wrong," the dejected salesclerk offered. We hit a charity shop that sold sample dresses at a discount and was run by a portly woman who was more drill sergeant that shopkeeper. "No bags. No shoes in the dressing room. Hang your dresses on this hook and wait your turn."

I had begun to lose hope when we arrived at a small bridal boutique on the Lower East Side. The store's owner, a cheerful woman named Debra, greeted us without much fanfare. When I told her my wedding date, she didn't balk. "That's doable," she said. She plucked a pile of dresses from the racks and led me to the changing room. She was heavily pregnant and when I asked her who would be doing alterations in the coming months, she said, "I own the shop and live upstairs, if you don't mind a screaming baby, I'll be doing them right here."

We narrowed the dozen frocks down to two: one that she had designed and one, which was much cheaper, from an outside designer. Rubbing her hand over her protruding belly, Debra tilted her head to the right. "Honestly," she said, "I think the cheaper one works better on you. You've got the height to pull it off."

It was a lovely dress, a simple ivory gown with Chinese buttons trailing down the back. "It's very elegant," said my mother. I had expected an "aha" moment, some sign that would tell me, *This is the one.* But instead, I was simply standing in a dress that looked pretty on, that I could afford, in a store where the owner would do the alterations for me at a reasonable price. Debra walked away, leaving my mother and me alone to talk.

"It's very pretty," my mom said.

"Isn't it . . ." I paused to think of just the right words to describe it, "simply stunning?"

SURVIVAL HINTS

1. When you're shopping for your wedding dress, shop around.
2. Don't get pushed into anything you don't love just because of time pressure and aggressive salespeople, and don't be afraid to say you need time to think about your decision. Remember that after all is said and done, you're the one who has to wear it!

The Bridal Net

Beth Ramsfield

NEVER IN MY wildest dreams did I imagine that my wedding planning would consist of hours—scratch that—*hundreds* of hours of Internet surfing. In the new millennium, brides can use the Internet to access just about anything we need to plan our weddings, and in ways our mothers could never have imagined. We can plan, book, and buy almost everything from thousands of online wedding sites, even the dress.

And so, with all these options at my fingertips, I became obsessed. I didn't realize it at first; in fact, it wasn't until *after* our wedding, when things had calmed down, that I realized I had become a wedding-site addict. (Yes, now I can say it out loud!) But I only realized how bad my addiction had gotten when I got back from my honeymoon and felt this incredible urge to go back and start surfing again. I even had a dream that I was still searching for a reception hall—days after the event was over!

In the months leading up to the wedding, I'd spent days staring at the screen, reading on discussion boards and in chat rooms what other brides were doing, finding out what was in vogue and what wasn't. Things got to such an extreme that before I realized it, I was so focused on surfing that I actually forgot to get moving on my own planning! I spent so much time online that I didn't do half the things I should have been doing at the appropriate time to prepare for the wedding, and I found myself slipping further and further behind. But surfing wedding sites to a new bride can be like chocolate to a chocoholic, liquor to an alcoholic, or Big Macs to a dieter.

I would rush home from work every day, toss my car keys on the table, not even pausing to take off my shoes, and head directly to the computer. Hitting that Enter button was like getting my fix. Soon it got so bad that at work I was skipping lunch to remain at my desk to surf even more wedding sites. I bounced from page to page and site to site, just to see what was new, and to be sure I didn't miss anything. Then I'd visit chat rooms and before long I was providing advice to other brides enmeshed in planning their weddings. Not that I was actually qualified to do this, considering that all I'd actually done was surf! But judging by the volume of thank-yous I received, I began to think I *was* an expert.

Where and when had the simple fun stopped? My general curiosity about searching for wedding options online had somehow transformed into a mission to create the wedding event of the century, the best of the best. I became so caught up in imagining the perfect day—with the most spectacular cake and band and flowers and food—that would outshine every other wedding in history, that I forgot all about what my fiancé and I had actually wanted in the first place, a quiet, intimate wedding with close family and friends. My surfing had made me intent on creating the trendy, talked-about wedding everyone would remember forever.

My fiancé finally brought the problem to my attention a few months before the wedding when he asked if I had booked the reception site yet. While I had made a great list of prospective sites, no, I still hadn't booked one. Then he asked if I had settled on the church or if the ceremony was going to be outside. And although I had also made a list of great prospective ceremony sites, I still hadn't decided on any of them either. Had I ordered the cake, and what about the flowers? I definitely had comprehensive lists for everything that I had found on the Internet, sometimes more than one list. I had even made file folders so I could easily sort through my various lists. But, what I hadn't done was book the reception, the church, or order the flowers or the cake. In other words, I'd done almost nothing at all, and with only a few months to go!

I had been so busy surfing and talking to other brides in chat rooms that I had completely lost track of my own. We didn't end up having the gala event of the year due to my online obsession, but we did have the lovely intimate affair we had pictured from the beginning.

As for Internet chat rooms, I steer clear of them these days. After all, I'm married now and have a lot of other things to think about. Besides, I'd much rather spend some quality time with my new husband than sit at the computer all night long.

SURVIVAL HINTS

1. The Internet provides a wealth of information for anyone planning a wedding. Just make sure to use it wisely and to not lose your own focus in the process.
2. Try making a schedule in order not to miss important cutoff dates for vendors or for ordering anything that may take a while. It'll save you a lot of grief later on.

The Inconvenient Wedding

Arline Simpson

IN SEPTEMBER OF 1963 I became engaged to my boss, and planning our wedding promised to be very exciting. Little did I know, however, that the play-off game of the season would coincide with our big day.

My boss/fiancé/soon-to-be husband decided that a mid-December wedding would work well because the Manhattan courts would be closed. (You guessed it, he is an attorney.) With a month picked for the wedding, the next thing I needed to focus on was finding a caterer and a place for the ceremony.

Fortunately, my dad's love was catering, and he knew the best hotels, restaurants, and caterers in Manhattan. So off we went, shopping for the perfect place for a December wedding.

After a few weekends of checking out places and comparing prices, I yielded to my sister's suggestion that we get married at the same temple and by the same rabbi who had officiated at her wedding. My fiancé and I made an appointment to meet him. He was very young and handsome, and he asked us about our respective families and talked about the ceremony. When I told the rabbi I wanted to get married in the sanctuary of the temple, he said "It's December; it could be snowing. Better I should wear the galoshes instead of the bride." Realizing he was right, that it was simpler to have the entire wedding, ceremony included, all in one place, I said, "OK, so I'll get married at the hotel where the reception will be."

We decided on a small hotel that sat right across the street from where my sister had had her wedding reception. The date was set and the place chosen. But my boss/fiancé/soon-to-be husband also was a New York Giants fanatic, and he and his friends had held season tickets since forever. Of all the luck, the Giants made it into the play-offs that year—and the game was scheduled for our wedding day!

Our ceremony was set for noon in Manhattan. The Giants game was at Yankee Stadium in the Bronx at exactly the same time. My boss/fiancé/soon-to-be husband asked if I could change the wedding location to the Concourse Plaza (in the Bronx of course—closer to the game!) and delay the ceremony to 6 P.M. instead of noon—so he could go to the game first! Well, that was an impossible request, of course, especially on such short notice, and this made him the target for all kinds of teasing from his friends for having to miss the big game.

The Saturday before the wedding day, my boss/ fiancé/soon-to-be husband and I visited a client who supplied us with the liquor for the big day, and then we went to Bloomingdale's to pick up my gown.

The day before the wedding, as we parked in front of the hotel, the doorman, a tall, red-cheeked, smiling Irish guy, came over and asked if he could help us unload. Gratefully, we said yes, and while he was unloading the trunk, he spun around to my fiancé and said, "Hey man, it looks like you're gonna have a helluva party!"

"No sir," said my fiancé, "we're getting married to-morrow." The tall, red-cheeked, and smiling Irish doorman replied, "It's no day to be getting married, man, it's a day to go to the game." I wanted to slug him!

Sunday arrived, and I was completely excited. The hotel gave me a small—very small—suite to change in, and my sister came up to help me dress. She also brought along a bottle of scotch. When I was in my gown, my hair and makeup done, my sister said, "Now you stay here till I come and get you because your hus-band can't see you until the ceremony." I had to miss the entire cocktail hour—and its delicious hors d'oeuvres—

because of that unfortunate tradition (one that luckily doesn't seem to be followed much anymore)!

So I sat all alone, in my gown, in that small—very small—suite, staring at myself in the mirror and wondering what was going on downstairs, and why no one was coming to get me. After about fifteen minutes of sheer frustration, boredom, and thirst, I took a drink. Another half hour passed. I took another one, and then another. I was almost in tears when my mom and sister came to get me—and more than a little light-headed and tipsy.

Getting ready to start the procession, I watched my sister and brother-in-law, respectively matron of honor and best man, as they walked down the aisle. I noticed my soon-to-be mother-in-law jump into the aisle and pull something out of my brother-in-law's ear: a transistor radio. The Giants were playing, and he was determined not to miss a play.

Mom and Dad each took my arm in theirs, kissed me, and smiled. I, giggling over my brother-in-law's radio, traipsed down the aisle, a happy, slightly tipsy bride.

We had a great time at the reception. That the men in the family kept running out to get a score did not stop us from having a wonderful, if not convenient, event, and despite everything, my husband and I have made it through forty-two years, with three children and four grandchildren.

And just for the record: The Giants won that play-off game, and still get into the play-offs once in a while!

SURVIVAL HINTS

1. With wedding plans, it's important to be flexible, but realistic, about how many activities or events you can fit into that day. Otherwise you'll be too busy running around to enjoy it.
2. Avoid drinking alcohol to excess before the ceremony, or you could end up being carried down the aisle!
3. No matter what, try to avoid scheduling your wedding during the World Series or NFL play-offs, and obviously avoid the Super Bowl at all costs, or you may end up with no groom or male guests in the dining room!

The One-Week Wedding

E. J. Toriello Fazio

IT WAS 1943, and my fiancé, who was in the army, was being shipped overseas during World War II. We'd known each other for six years by then, and knew we would always be together. But now that he was being sent to war, and who knew when—or even if—he'd ever come home, we decided to take the plunge.

What do you do with only one week to pull a wedding together? I rushed to the bridal shop so I could be fitted for the one dress they had that was in my size, size 2, and it actually looked good. It was white organza with a long train and about fifty covered buttons running all the way down the back. It had puffy sleeves, and the veil was a pointed tiara made of seed pearls. I was lucky that they matched, too! I could only choose from what was in stock at the store—no chance of ordering anything else with only one week's notice!

Next came the shoes. I had the smallest feet of anyone I knew, size 4, and there was very little to choose from. I ended up with open-toe, pierced white leather high-heel shoes, a necessity because my husband-to-be was a full foot taller than I was. The shoes looked like they belonged on a nurse, but who cared? They'd be mostly covered by the wedding dress anyway, and at least they fit and were white.

Our original best man, my brother, was overseas already, stationed somewhere in Italy, and nobody knew where, so my cousin Ben took his place. Joe, my husband, wore his army uniform, and my maid of honor, Frances, wore one of her own dresses.

We arranged things with the church, which wasn't all that simple because we had to turn up two sets of baptismal certificates, one set from New York City, where my fiancé was born. We were to be married in my local parish, in the town where I was born, but with my cousin Bill, who was a priest, officiating. Most of the remaining details were quickly handled, as were the blood tests.

Finally, everything was set, and my older brother agreed to drive us to the church in his big new black car. After the ceremony, we were to go back to my parents' house, a big gray three-story Victorian, where the celebration and reception would be held.

Or so we thought.

As we came out of the church and were being congratulated by everyone, my father-in-law came up to us and said, tensely, "You have to come back to my house for a while. Everyone's there waiting for you!"

I was surprised, wondering why they hadn't gone to my parents' house, but we agreed. Really, what else could we do at that point? The plans had been made so quickly that there was obviously a mix-up about the venue. All the while I wondered, Who hijacks the bridal couple on the way to their own reception? And by half the relatives who were invited and were expected along with all the other guests? But we went, in the opposite direction of the official reception, only to be delayed considerably by the houseful of relatives from all over New York and Connecticut, among other places. At last we were able to get away.

When we arrived at my parents' house, everyone was wondering where we'd disappeared to and why half the guests were missing. What could we say? We didn't expect to have two separate receptions, but we couldn't do anything about it at that point. We just told them what had happened and went to greet the rest of our guests.

We had a wonderful homemade buffet dinner, complete with all kinds of Italian delicacies that my parents and family had prepared, followed by coffee and a wedding cake. We had a great time, with the wisecracks and jokes coming thick and fast from my father, my husband, and Cousin Benny.

We'd actually considered eloping, but hadn't wanted to disappoint our families. Considering the confusion and chaos over the reception, maybe we should have stuck to our plan. In the end, however, we had a really wonderful time.

After our reception, we left for the weekend honeymoon at The Lincoln Hotel in New York City. All appeared to be going as planned until the last mishap of our barely planned wedding. It happened on the way to the city. My sister-in-law had been using my husband's car while he was in the service, but on our way to our hotel, we found that she had left barely a drop of gas in the car!

Driving oneself to the honeymoon is a far cry from today's dependence on limousines. At the last possible second, just as the car was stalling out, we rolled into a gas station. There my husband, still in uniform, was saluted by the attendant, who thought he was an officer. Because this was wartime, we paid for the gas with gas-rationing coupons donated by my father. Finally we arrived at the hotel, as arranged for us by the ever-resourceful Cousin Ben.

After the all-too-brief overnight honeymoon, on Sunday night the groom had to report back to the base in Massachusetts. He came home one more time, practically on his way to shipping out of Connecticut on the HMS *Slaughterdyke,* a British troop ship, and his two-year adventure in Africa and Europe began.

I, on the other hand, worked in my father's office and waited to get letters from overseas until Joey returned in 1945. We were married for fifty-eight years.

SURVIVAL HINTS

1. Sometimes your wedding plans don't go as expected, so don't be thrown when it happens to you.
2. If an in-law throws you a curve, be flexible, because you'll be dealing with them for the rest of your life and your wedding day is no time for a showdown.

Sometimes Late *Is* Better

Ziggy Caruso

I WAS RUNNING late that hot July Saturday when I was due at the church for my friend's wedding, and despite the good directions, I got distracted and made a wrong turn somewhere along the way. Eventually I found the street, and when I finally arrived at the church, a few moments before the appointed time, I noticed an un-usual number of sweaty-looking people milling about on the parish grounds. "Hmm," I thought, "I wonder why they're all outside at this hour? The wedding should be starting right about now."

I spotted some friends of the bride I knew well, and found out that the beautiful little country church had no air-conditioning, hence the sweating guests. Not only that, but the bride hadn't yet arrived. Tradition dictates that the bride should be a little bit late, so no-body was too concerned at first. We were all happily chatting despite the 99-degree heat. It was a joyful occa-sion, and we were all so happy for this couple who had met later in life, had had a fairy-tale romance, and now a wedding.

While we waited outside, I spoke to the bride's brother, one of my closest friends, who was to walk her down the aisle. He was hot in his tuxedo, and the sun was reflecting off his shades. He looked like someone out of *The Sopranos,* and probably so did I. Finally we wanted to sit down, and we had no choice but to go in-side the sweltering little church.

Inside, the church was tiny, but packed with people in every single seat. There we sat in our wedding finery, melting in the heat, wondering if we'd be mere puddles by the time the pictures were taken. Well after the sched-uled hour for the wedding came and went, we began to wonder what was going on.

Seated with several of the bride's lifelong girlfriends, I could barely keep from passing out. Finally, none of us could take the heat. We walked outside again to get a breath of air, when I noticed that the two members of the clergy, an Episcopal minister and a Catholic priest, had also left the altar, exiting through the side door, and were heading to the rectory. Hmm again. We milled around some more, and then finally the bride, her sister, and her brother-in-law arrived, over forty-five minutes late. But the bride looked radiant and stunning in her gown, her tan offset by the lovely, creamy, satin fabric.

We all happily returned to our seats, and for a while, nothing happened. The minister and priest had not yet reentered the church. At last they reappeared through the side door, took their places, nodded to each other, and the string quartet began to play.

The bride walked down the aisle on her brother's arm, and the ceremony began. The minister told us that waiting, although sometimes frustrating, can be the most important time for us spiritually, and that the events of that very day were proof of this fact.

Apparently the two clergy members had never met until that day, and the fact that the bride was detained gave them time to work out the differences in their beliefs, dogma, practices, and approaches, based on the stipulations of their two branches of Christianity. Because they had had enough time to work things out between them, the minister invited the Catholic priest, who had not been scheduled to do anything but bless the couple after the ceremony, to concelebrate the wedding with her in a joint rite. It was a surprising turn of events, and the bride, a life-long devout Catholic, was thrilled by this unexpected gift.

We never did find out why the bride was so late, but thanks to her delay, along with the gracious generosity of the two clergy, there was a little extra sweetness to the icing on her wedding cake.

SURVIVAL HINTS

1. Be patient if you're kept waiting at a wedding. Sometimes something wonderful and unexpected may come of it.
2. When people with open hearts and generous attitudes connect, magic can happen.

2

When You're Planning a Destination Wedding or an Unconventional Venue

The Floating Wedding: Or, How Not to Plan the Big Event
Mark Eisenstein

The Wedding Countdown Clock
Gloria Rose Mello

Planning Our Renaissance Wedding
Brian J. P. Craig

The Wedding in Mumbai
Joy Tansin

A Wedding in Italy
Judy Caruso

Sanity Quiz

You're marrying a great guy who also happens to be a die-hard cowboy, which is what attracted you to him in the first place. But now it's time to plan your wedding and he insists the entire wedding party be on horseback for the ceremony.

Do you
A. say ride 'em cowboy and go for the gusto
B. tell him it's a bit much but you'll do it anyway
C. refuse for yourself but let him go on horseback
D. trade in your dress for a pair of chaps

Whether you picked A, B, C, or D, you clearly can learn from our contributors. Read on and laugh!

The Floating Wedding: Or, How *Not* to Plan the Big Event

Mark Eisenstein

I WILL ADMIT, it seemed like a good idea at the time. A romantic trip to the Bahamas was already in the works . . . what better excuse for a wedding and a honeymoon?

Brian, my old college roommate, called me just three weeks before his and Lacey's planned trip to the Bahamas and ran the wedding idea by me. I had shared my apartment briefly with these two the previous year and had known then that their getting married was inevitable. My first reaction was, sure, why not. "Just do it," I said, "and I'll be there as your best man."

I hung up the phone, wrote the date on my calendar—and that's when it hit me. OK, I was single at the time and didn't have much experience with these things, but don't weddings take months, even a full year or longer, to plan? And this was happening in three weeks? Well, maybe Brian and Lacey knew something I didn't, and how difficult could it be anyway? Some family, a few friends, a few vows, a few drinks, and voila . . . they would be off to the Bahamas!

The date was set, and the venue planned, but where the actual ceremony would be held was still up in the air. Brian always had a thing for boats and Lacey's family lived on a major resort lake in the White Mountains of New Hampshire, so they came up with the great idea of having the wedding on an excursion boat. That's right—not a ship—a boat! The "ship" was not available that weekend, but the boat, a small double-deck lake ferry, was. The wedding would be a memorable "three-hour tour."

As I planned to tie this trip together with a few days off of my own, I headed north, packed for a relaxing, easy, long weekend. Bathing suit, tennis garb, sweater for the cool late spring evenings, casual slacks and shirt, and . . . where was the suit? I could have sworn I'd hung that suit in the back seat. Of course, I only realized that I hadn't actually taken it along late in the afternoon the day before the wedding!

Now, I'd seen the ads for Gentleman's Warehouse, where the poor guy's business suit is splattered with mud while waiting for a cab in Manhattan, and they miraculously keep the store open to select and fit him for the next day's meeting, but I wasn't in Manhattan. I was just west of "East Bumstruck" somewhere, and the only store still open at 4:30 P.M. on a Saturday was Lou's Menswear and Fishing Tackle. (Seems like every store in New Hampshire, no matter what their main line, sells fishing tackle, along with maple syrup and moccasins.) And, of course, they didn't accept American Express!

Surprisingly, the selection wasn't too bad, and, after pleading with the salesman to accept a personal out-of-state check, and to have the slacks shortened on the spot, I left with my suit and a complimentary bottle of maple syrup (eight ounces free with every purchase of one hundred dollars or more!) for the rehearsal dinner at Lacey's parents' home.

No sooner had I arrived at the house than I found Lacey frazzled and exhausted, an emotional wreck. Her mother trailed behind her, dressed (at least partially) in a yellow gown that dated from her last formal event, her other daughter's wedding ten years earlier. Mom was trying to explain that it was not her fault; that the gown seemed to have shrunk about three sizes while in storage, and how was she to know it would be a bit "snug"?

Soon the bride packed Mom and a few girlfriends into her tiny car and off they went to find another dress at the big department store, Rob's Fashion Emporium and Hardware, in the county seat about an hour away. Later that evening, while we dined on roast beef, roasted potatoes, various veggies, and our friend Edie's mom's famous dark chocolate layer cake sent along for the occasion, Lacey and her sister sewed, fitted, sewed, fitted, and finally stuffed Mom into her new gown, ready for the following day's big event.

The wedding was to be a late afternoon affair, with the sun slowly setting over the lake, adding tiny golden reflections dancing on calm waters to bring true romance to the event. The ceremony itself would be held on the boat's upper deck, under a deepening blue sky and gentle lake breeze. Actually, the weather seemed to be holding nicely that day, a little windy but, at four in the afternoon, when we all clambered aboard the vessel, the sun was shining with only a slight wisp of cumulus clouds overhead.

Well, there's an expression in New England: "If you don't like the weather, wait ten minutes." And in New Hampshire, with its mountains and trees, anything looming on the horizon goes unseen until it's directly overhead. As luck would have it, as soon as the boat lines were released and we were under way, the clouds moved in. While they were noticed by all on board (all except the blissful couple) the lake seemed calm enough and our attention was turned to the big event.

Musically, many pieces would have worked: the first movement of Dvorak's First Symphony, the Adagio in E Flat by Mozart, even "Sunrise, Sunset" from *Fiddler on the Roof* have been used to set the mood at many weddings I've attended. Brian had left this responsibility to Lacey's younger brother, who diligently recorded and played back selections approved by the loving couple. Unfortunately, he also recorded, on the flip side of the tape, "In-A-Gadda-Da-Vida" by Iron Butterfly, which blared over the boat's raspy PA system as we left the dock. This went on for at least five minutes as the wheelhouse holding the PA system could not hear what was blasting out of it. While the crowd on shore, most of whom were under the age of twenty, rollicked with this impromptu concert (sound really does travel a long way over water!) most on board had no idea what this noise was. Finally someone in the wheelhouse noticed the error and we sailed into a cloudy sunset to the strains of Zero Mostel's Tevya crooning "Sunrise, Sunset" after all.

At last, with the music corrected, dresses and suits properly in place on all parties, and clouds gathering overhead while the New York deli buffet waited for us on the lower deck, the ceremony finally got started. This was to be an interfaith marriage, and we had the only available rabbi—they're not so easy to find in New Hampshire. I hadn't thought of why Brian had chosen music from *Fiddler on the Roof* until I realized that the rabbi may have been old enough to be Tevya's brother. The priest, a very articulate young man who knew the bride's family well, spoke eloquently about the meaning of love, the binding of spirits but not souls, and so on and so on, to the point that the rabbi, who had evidently missed his afternoon nap, started to nod off.

After some gentle prodding by the, ahem, best man (we were a very "close" group on this upper deck), the rabbi started in with his own dissertation. It was agreed that the rabbi would perform the actual ceremony and it started out quite well. And, if the groom's name had been John instead of Brian, it would have gone off without a hitch. How the names could have gotten mixed up no one knows, but it was "John . . . do you take . . . ." Well, you get the idea.

No sooner had the rabbi finally figured out that John was from last week's ceremony, than the skies opened up. I had fleeting thoughts then that maybe this union just wasn't meant to be. All hands scurried below deck and there, between the deli meats on the left and the coleslaw and potato salad on the right, we finalized what would be a long and happy . . . . But wait, why were the engines slowing? No, they'd stopped, a full stop, in the rain, in the middle of the lake!

Suddenly, a small craft pulled alongside our bobbing celebration and over the rail came a young lady bearing two large floral arrangements and a box of bouquets, boutonnieres, and corsages. Yes, the florist had finally caught up to the wedding party and was determined to deliver the goods!

Along with the two large bouquets for the bride and matron of honor were the centerpieces for the buffet, and as all hands aided in passing the centerpieces from one boat to another, Brian and Lacey stood just to the right of the kosher chicken wings, blissful in their moment.

Ask them today, twenty-seven years later, what they remember most about the three-hour tour and they smile, hold hands, and say, "Did you catch that sunset?"

It just proves that the sages were right: love truly is blind.

SURVIVAL HINTS

1. If you decide to organize a last-minute wedding, be flexible.
2. Try to give everyone as much notice as possible because even the simplest wedding takes a lot of planning.
3. Be ready for anything, because any event can have mix-ups, and a last-minute wedding is practically guaranteed to have things go wrong.

The Wedding Countdown Clock

Gloria Rose Mello

IT ALL STARTED on our engagement day, February 14, 2005, when Beth, a very dear friend of ours, gave us a Wedding Day Countdown Clock as an engagement gift. Every day my fiancé and I would check the day, hour, minute, and second of the countdown. As the hours ticked by, we couldn't wait to see what the clock would do on our big day.

Our plan was to be married on the beach at sunrise in Hawaii on Valentine's Day, 2006. We were going to fly from New Jersey to Hawaii on the Saturday before our Tuesday wedding, so that meant that in order for us to see what the pretty little countdown clock did, we had to pack it and take it along with us. Easier said than done.

When I mentioned this to my son (from my previous marriage), his reply was, "Mom, they will not only confiscate the clock at the airport, but you will be *arrested*. When they see the X-ray of your bag and inside is something that is counting down to the last second . . . they may think that it's a *bomb* and you're a *terrorist!*"

I had watched this pretty little countdown clock for almost a whole year, and the idea of now leaving it at home right before the event was just not going to happen. So, on the day before we were to leave for our trip, off I went to mail the package.

"This *must* arrive at our hotel in Hawaii on Monday so that we're sure to have it in time for our wedding the next day," I told the woman behind the counter. She smiled, weighed my little package, and said, "This is going to cost you one hundred dollars to send it the cheapest way, via express overnight." I nearly fainted.

"Even if you decided to ship this out today," she continued, "there is no guarantee that you will get it in time. If we get that blizzard as they are predicting, there is a very good chance that *all* flights may be grounded and your package will be delayed." Now I was really feeling sick.

I wasn't worried about our flight, as ours was in the early part of the day and the storm wasn't expected to hit until later that afternoon. But what was I going to do about the clock? I really wanted to see what my countdown clock did every last day until the wedding, and I wasn't about to leave it behind with someone else so that they could tell me later what the clock actually did on our wedding day.

"Can I make a suggestion?" the woman asked.

"Sure, I'm all ears," I said.

"Why don't you get a wedding gift bag, place the clock in it, put tissue paper in it, and take it as your carry-on? If they ask you about it you can tell them that it's a wedding present. You really have nothing to lose at this point. I travel a lot and I really don't think that they will confiscate it. You wouldn't be able to listen to it if they took it anyway, so why not give it a try?"

"Okay," I said. So I did as she suggested and put the clock into a wedding gift bag.

The day arrived for us to leave New Jersey and head to the airport for our wedding/honeymoon in Hawaii as planned. I had already had my hair done up for the wedding the way Bob, my sweetheart, likes it, and I was all set to fight with security at the airport if they gave me any trouble over my clock. We got to the airport security station and I placed my carry-on luggage on the conveyor belt along with my "wedding gift." Everything went through without a hitch.

Now all I had to do was walk through the metal detector and pick up my belongings. But not so fast: As I walked through the arches, the machine starting beeping like crazy. The security guards pulled me aside and had me stand with my arms outstretched, shoes off and feet apart. They proceeded to wave the wand over my entire body, until it began beeping at my bracelets. Then the security guard asked me if I had any hairpins in my hair.

"Do I have any hairpins? Only about fifty or so!" I said.

Having my hair done up in curls required dozens of hairpins to keep it looking great until the ceremony. After they patted me down and did another wand check, they finally let me go through and get my belongings. One down and one more to go! Our flight was directly to Hawaii, but we were getting married in Kauai and that meant another flight. I was tickled that my package made it through one airport, but I wasn't sure about the next one. All I could do was pray.

Ten hours later, we landed in Honolulu and spent the night there because the last shuttle flight of the night to the island of Kauai had just left. We got up early that next morning, Sunday, and took the hotel shuttle bus to the airport.

At the security checkpoint, I placed all of my belongings on the conveyor belt and held my breath. No one said anything—we were home free! We took the twenty-five-minute flight to Kauai and arrived at our hotel all in one piece. We unpacked and notified our wedding planner that we had arrived; she told us where to go to get our marriage license on Monday.

That morning, off we went to Pono Market. That was all she told us: "Look for Pono Market and get your license there. I've made you an appointment with Kevin." After driving for about a half an hour, through the center of the town filled with many stores and businesses, I finally spotted a storefront that read Pono Market.

"Pull over!" I screamed. "There's Pono Market!"

We parked the car and walked to the place where I had seen the sign. On the facade of the building there was another sign that read, Marriage Licenses Sold Here. We opened the door only to discover . . . a deli! Could this possibly be the right place?

We had an 11:30 A.M. appointment to obtain our license. At first we thought it was a joke, but when we asked for Kevin, a nice Hawaiian gentleman came forward and introduced himself. We stood there, filled out forms, and gave them to Kevin, who took off with them up a spiral staircase to the next floor. It seemed like an eternity before he came back—I was ready to order a sandwich and a soda!

Eventually he came back down the stairs with our official marriage license. He took our picture and inserted it into one of two albums that he showed us, which included shots of about a thousand couples he had given licenses to in the past year alone. Kevin also gave us a bumper sticker that read: I got my Marriage License at Pono Market, Hawaii.

Now the license was taken care of. Tomorrow would be the Big Day, and we could barely wait. After having a romantic dinner, my sweetheart went to his room and I retired to mine. After all, he wasn't supposed to see me the night before the wedding, right?

But I couldn't sleep all night. I was afraid my carefully pinned up hair was going to be ruined if I slept on it, so I had to prop myself up on all the pillows—very uncomfortable, but, I figured, well worth it.

Finally, Tuesday, February 14, 2006, dawned: my wedding day! Bob, my sweetheart, called me at 4 A.M. to make sure I was up, and then called me again at 6:45 A.M. when the limo arrived. Our wedding was to be at 8 A.M., and the beach where we'd have the ceremony was about an hour away.

Dressed in my gown, I grabbed my special wedding gift along with the rings before leaving my room. At this point I had the countdown clock out of its bag as the minutes were now counting down rapidly. I had to make it up the escalator to get to the front of the hotel where my honey and the limo were waiting.

Traveling up the escalator, I looked up and spotted my sweetheart waiting at the very top, looking down at me and taking my picture. I started to get a little weepy, but there was no time for that: Our clock was counting down . . . thirty-seven seconds, thirty-six seconds . . . and I was still on the escalator with the clock ticking down to twenty-five seconds.

I got off the escalator and greeted my honey with a kiss, and before we knew it, we were counting down the seconds. The few people around us started to count down with us, even though they had no idea what they were counting down for. It was just like the New Year's Eve ball drop in Times Square. After waiting an entire year, the long-awaited final countdown was taking place.

With so much anticipation, we all were shouting, ten, nine, eight, seven, six, five, four, *three, two, one!* And what did our pretty little countdown clock do? It started flashing all zeros. . . . That's right. It just kept flashing zeros and more zeros. We picked it up and held it to our ears to see if maybe it was too noisy in the lobby for us to hear it playing something like the wedding march, or Ta Daaaaaa! Or something, but no.

We looked at each other in total disbelief. The pretty little countdown clock did absolutely *nothing* but count down to zero. We looked at each other again, laughed hysterically, gave each other a kiss, and said, "Come on, let's get married!"

We got into our white stretch limo and did just that. I tossed that pretty little countdown clock out the window and proceeded to our sunrise wedding on the beach in Kauai. I suppose I should tell you about the wedding . . . but that's another story.

SURVIVAL HINTS

1. If your wedding is out of town in an exotic location, think before you pack anything of sentimental value that might end up being confiscated. If you can, mail it ahead to save yourself trauma at the airport.
2. Leave plenty of extra time if your wedding is somewhere unfamiliar, in case you have to do any last-minute running around for licenses or forms.
3. Don't be surprised by anything you encounter outside your local area. Sometimes everything is done a little bit differently.

Planning Our Renaissance Wedding

Brian J. P. Craig

FOR A WHILE, it seemed I'd never find the right girl and get married. But I figured that if I did, it would be a normal tux-and-white-dress wedding. I certainly had no desire for a theme wedding. It's funny how things work out.

Soon after Barbara and I started dating, we began teasing each other about getting married. One of us would say something about "when we're married" or "after we're married," and Barbara would say, "That's assuming that you ask me." I'd reply, "And assuming that you say yes!"

One thing we shared was a love for Renaissance Faires. One day we were walking around New York City, when I suddenly said, "Hey, you know what would be fun, assuming I ask you and assuming you say yes? We should have a Renaissance wedding!" I don't know where the idea came from, but Barbara agreed and we promptly went on to other topics of conversation.

Eventually, I did ask, and she did say yes, and we found that we really liked the idea of a Renaissance wedding. It would be different, fun, and romantic. Besides, I come from an extended Irish family and had been to weddings for what seemed like nine thousand cousins. They were all nice, but after a while they started to blend together. I wanted to do something that people would remember! Neither of us was an historian or a Renaissance expert, so we weren't worried about authenticity. But we wanted our special day to have as many elements as possible of the Renaissance Faires that we loved.

At the time we were attending a Unitarian church housed in a thirty-five-room mansion that had been converted from a turn-of-the-century silver baron's summer cottage. It wasn't quite a castle, but it had a wonderful historic atmosphere, and we wouldn't think of being married by anyone but our minister. We reserved the date, and the plans for our Renaissance wedding began.

The first family member we hit with the news was my mother. We were out shopping with her and discussing the wedding when I told her, "We decided to do our wedding with a bit of a Renaissance twist."

I've got to hand it to my mother. My younger brother had eloped a few years earlier, so I think she was looking forward to being part of a nice traditional wedding. Still, she didn't freak out like I half expected. She paused for a moment and then calmly said. "Oh. Okay . . . . Why?"

We explained that we wanted to do something fun and different, so she sighed and accepted it. When we asked if she wanted to wear Renaissance garb, she said she'd have to think it over. My two brothers (the groomsmen), and Barbara's friend and her cousin (the bridesmaids), would be in costume, but we figured the six of us would be the only ones to dress in authentic garb. Neither of us expected our parents to wear Renaissance clothes.

Barbara's mom had passed away a few years before we met. Because of that, and because my mother wasn't involved in my brother's wedding, my mother wanted to help with the planning. So, when one of the clothing vendors from the Renaissance Faire was hosting an open house, we all went to look at the selection in their warehouse.

Barbara and I both found outfits that we liked, and we had decided to use the colors of my family crest as our wedding colors: red, white, black, and silver. Barbara mentioned that she wanted her dress in red.

"Oh, I'm sorry," one of the saleswomen told her. "We have some rusts and oranges, but we really don't work much with red."

The other said, "Wait . . . we did just get in a bolt of red fabric in two-tone harlequin pattern. Dale wasn't sure why he ordered it, so it's just sitting on the shelf!"

Sure enough, when we talked to the manager, he confirmed that they had just gotten a red harlequin fabric that would be perfect for Barbara's dress. Moreover, they also got a matching black harlequin fabric that would work for my outfit. He had no idea why he had ordered any of it, other than that it had looked interesting in the catalog.

On the drive home, Barbara said, "You know what? I think my mother was looking out to make sure we got what we needed for the wedding." My mother and I agreed; somehow it was the only thing that made sense to us.

We started attending bridal shows to get ideas, and talked to some photographers, none of whom impressed us. Luckily, a friend at work had gotten married the year before and gave me the name of the photographer he used. Barbara and I met him and liked him immediately. Besides, he was much more reasonably priced than anyone else we had talked to.

Both the ceremony and the reception would be at the Unitarian church. We decided to have the dinner out on the terrace, and reserve the room next to it for dancing. My youngest brother worked for a DJ company at the time, and recommended a coworker. We found a caterer who would handle the cocktail hour and part of the meal, as well as supply tables, chairs, linens, and a tent for the terrace. For the rest of the meal, we wanted something different, so we ordered food from one of our favorite Indian restaurants as well as some Italian dishes from the caterer.

We were surprised at how smoothly the planning was going. But nothing was as surprising as when my mother called. "I decided that I wanted to dress up in period garb for the wedding," she said. "And I told your father he should do it, too."

My father probably wasn't too hard to convince. He's very active in the Elks, and had, over the years, dressed up as an Italian priest and a member of the Supremes for various fund-raisers. We told them that we'd take them back to the place that we liked to look at outfits. Then Barbara called her father and told him that my folks were dressing up. She asked if he wanted to come along and look at some outfits, too. Barbara's father is a bit more reserved than my father (hell, Jerry Lewis is a bit more reserved than my father), but he agreed to come and look.

My mom quickly found a dress she liked. My father was a bit tougher, but I eventually found him an outfit with a floppy hat. As I handed it to him, I said, "Try this. You don't have to wear the hat if you don't want to."

My father's face lit up. "I get to wear a hat?" He plopped the floppy hat on his head and looked in the mirror. Without even trying on the rest of the outfit, he said, "Oh, this is the one!"

Barbara's dad was the hardest of all. The only outfit that he liked was one for an executioner. "Can I come as the executioner?" he asked. I think he was half joking and half hoping that we'd say no so that he wouldn't have to dress up. But I said, "Charlie, if you like the executioner outfit, you can wear it and carry a big axe."

We later found two other places that custom-made Renaissance clothing, and they supplied the outfits for our bridal party. One of the costume shops had a terrific outfit that we recommended to our minister. He seemed unsure at first, but said that he thought he could pull it off. My niece, who was five at the time, was going to be our flower girl. She already had a simple white dress, so we ordered her a pair of pink fairy wings and a flowered tiara.

At the Renaissance Faire that year, we had already bought wooden swords for my brothers and me, along with our gifts for the bridal party: a castle-shaped unity candle, and the wedding issue of *Renaissance Magazine*. In it we saw a picture of a woman carrying a scepter instead of the usual bouquet. Barbara's dad said he could make scepters like that, so I got him the wood and he did a fabulous job. Barbara spent one day painting and decorating them with fake gems, lace, and imitation ivy. All we needed now was a cake!

We found a cake artist online, then met with her to describe the cake of our dreams: a colorful confection designed to look like a castle sitting atop a hill. She drew a quick sketch that seemed to capture what we wanted, then we signed the contract and gave her a deposit.

One fun aspect of getting married by a Unitarian minister is that Unitarians don't have a set rite, so we got to write our own ceremony. We borrowed bits from various wedding ceremonies that we found online and in books. We were very happy with our vows (which we recite to each other on our anniversary), and were curious to see if anyone would say anything about the line where we promised each other, "Yours will be the name

I cry out in the night." Either everyone missed it, or they didn't quite know what to say!

On the day of the wedding, right before the ceremony was to begin, the cake hadn't yet arrived. We started to panic. Barbara tried calling the baker, leaving a message with her cell phone number. Unfortunately, she then handed her purse—with the phone inside, ringer on—to my mother to hold during the ceremony. Naturally, the baker called back in the middle of the ceremony! My mother didn't know how to shut off Barbara's cell phone, so she just tried to muffle the noise till it stopped. Afterward we all had a laugh over it, since everyone in the chapel had heard the phone ring, but nobody ever expected that it belonged to the bride.

After the ceremony, the bar was open and the drink fountains were turned on. The wait staff, who loved our theme, had claimed some extra decorations and had clipped some ivy from outside to decorate their serving trays. The cake at last showed up, and some of the guests got a bit of a show as they watched it being assembled. The cake turned out to be mostly white with a few colored decorations, instead of the colorful display we had expected, but it still tasted good. Later, I checked the paperwork and realized that, despite all our talk, the baker hadn't made any notations about the colors on either the contract or the sketch.

Barbara's dad wore a billowing grey shirt and slacks under the fancy black leather vest from the executioner's outfit. It worked very well, and he looked good in the pictures. Although he didn't admit it, I think he kind of enjoyed the outfit.

My folks had a blast posing in their outfits. To our delight, quite a few of our guests came in costume as well, at least a third of them, and my father took it as a personal challenge to try on every hat he could. The photographer, who did a great job, got several shots of my father's haberdashery trophies.

When all was said and done, our fairy-tale Renaissance wedding was a success. And now, a few years later, people are still talking about it.

SURVIVAL HINTS

1. Have fun with the planning, because if you can't enjoy the wedding, you'll have a hard time enjoying the marriage.
2. Do what you want. It's *your* wedding, after all. And when you follow your heart, things will most likely work out well.
3. Make sure *every* detail is in the contract, no matter how small.
4. Hire people you enjoy being with. You don't want to ruin an important and beautiful day by having some jerk playing the wrong music or knocking people over to take pictures.

The Wedding in Mumbai

Joy Tansin

I WAS VERY fortunate last year to be invited to a lavish wedding in India in July. The bride and groom were very close friends, so I was thrilled to be included in the guest list. To my delight, we were all to fly together from the United States to New Delhi, and I would be a guest at the bride's home. I had helped her with some of the state-side planning, but had no idea what was going to happen once we got to India.

The couple took me on a weeklong sightseeing trip before the wedding celebration—the country is astonishing in breadth, sights, culture, and variety, not to mention the vast crowds of humanity. This is something that can only be appreciated by actually visiting India, and no amount of reading, video viewing, or photos can ever do it justice.

And little did I know how much I'd become a part of the family whose home was overflowing with guests. I was immediately accommodated in one of the precious few beds while most of the family slept on the floor of the average-sized house. I was given every possible comfort out of deference for my non-Indian heritage, and felt both guilty and thrilled to be treated as such an honored guest. Not only that, but I was encouraged to help with opinions and ideas on the details of preparation whenever possible, which was no doubt done to make me feel like part of the family. It gave me an unexpected and unusual inside view of the planning, and we all got to know each other.

Staying there in the bride's family home, I was able to witness the amazing preparations for this lavish three-day celebration, the most interesting of which involved the face- and hand-painting of the bride and other female participants, along with the other preparations. Best of all, I was given the most exquisite red silk sari as my wedding costume, along with lessons on how to wrap and wear it. It had to be the most comfortable dress I've ever worn, especially at a wedding in blistering heat.

At last the day of the wedding arrived. The gorgeously dressed groom arrived at the bride's house, which was decorated in colorful trappings, accompanied by his entire entourage of family and friends. They were led to the tents set up for the celebration, and the elaborate ceremony began. The bride asked me to make a special offering of incense as an honored guest, and we both got teary when we bowed to each other. After three hours of joyful ritual, prayer, chanting, and music, with people casually coming and going, talking and visiting, moving about, and smiling and laughing the entire time, the couple was officially married. At last they led all of their guests to the feast.

A lifelong fan of Indian food, I never before had seen such an array of dishes and foods. It was a heavenly selection I'll never forget. The bride had asked me for a list of my favorite dishes just to be sure I'd like something, but it was all sublime. We celebrated with music and dancing that night, and then the partying continued for two additional days, each one bringing new and extraordinary culinary and musical offerings.

Finally, the last of the parties came to an end. The next day, it was time to return home, exhausted, sated, and happy. The bride kept thanking me for all my help with the preparations, but it really was nothing compared to their families' efforts to create such an amazing celebration.

After my adventure in India, no other wedding is likely to ever seem as rich in spectacle or length, and it was my great privilege to have been included in all the joy-filled festivities in honor of the lovely young couple.

SURVIVAL HINTS

1. If you're planning a wedding in a foreign country, be sure to let your guests know in advance what to expect from a culture that differs from their own, to ensure that they have the best possible new experiences, without any misunderstandings regarding local customs and practices.

2. If you're inviting guests to a wedding in a culture that's foreign to them, let them know what's expected as a guest to avoid embarrassment on their part and to make them feel as at home as possible.

A Wedding in Italy

Judy Caruso

PEOPLE HAVE ALWAYS married outside their faiths, countries, and cultures, and historically this was how treaties and alliances were made, as well as new families formed. In my own family, we've had only one offshore wedding so far, when my aunt got married in Italy—to a man she'd never even met before! It wasn't exactly an arranged marriage, but there was some "fixing up," at least on the part of the groom's brother, and the resulting wedding involved a tremendous amount of planning, both here and overseas.

Of course, there was the mandatory lengthy shopping trip to find the expensive and gorgeously elaborate beaded and lacy wedding gown, which took a long time to make and which needed all kinds of fittings so that it was perfect. My aunt was excited and happy; her wedding was going to be quite a romantic adventure.

My aunt was in her thirties and still single—she'd had her choice of men, but never ended up settling down with any of them. In many ways she was ahead of her time. She had worked and saved for many years, had a nice car and clothes, and a slew of nieces and nephews who loved her. She was independent. But then one day she met Gulio, a coworker, who told her about his brothers in Italy. Small in stature, Gulio was attractive and suave—just the kind of man a woman could fall for. But since he was married, and since he liked my aunt, he decided to do some matchmaking on behalf of his brother.

Soon Gulio's brother and my aunt were corresponding frequently and, after a time, Augustino wrote to my aunt proposing marriage—and she accepted.

But after months of planning, one major detail was yet to be decided. Who was going where for the wedding? Partly due to immigration laws, it was suggested that my aunt travel abroad for the wedding and return with her new husband in tow, who would then be a legal entrant to the States, where they planned to live.

The next item: Who would accompany the bride to Italy? My grandmother declined to go on the trip because she felt it inappropriate for the bride to travel for the wedding, immigration laws be damned; the man should be the one to travel for the wedding. And since the groom wasn't coming here to be married, his mother-in-law would stay home in protest. And *her* word was final.

But still, someone from the family had to go along, both as a witness and to represent the family, since it was too expensive for the whole clan to go along on the trip. After much negotiation and argument, it was settled: My father would go. Naturally, my mother was not sending him off to Italy alone, so she too became part of the U.S. wedding party delegation.

I was deemed too young to go along. My father was adamant that rural postwar Italy wasn't in great shape and would be too rough for a child. Dad had been stationed all over Italy during World War II and knew well the poor conditions of some of the outlying rural areas there. Knowing that the groom's hometown was in a tiny mountain village in southern Italy, Dad was not taking his only child to a place that most likely had no modern conveniences. This turned out to be not only wise, but also a major understatement.

Upon their arrival, my parents and aunt were met at the airport by the prospective groom and his brother, who had arrived in a tiny Fiat with room for only two people. My aunt apparently approved of her fiancé, now that she saw him in the flesh, because she agreed to go on with the planned wedding. But eyewitnesses recount that my father, a large Sicilian complete with a legendary temper, was apoplectic at the sight of the car, never mind the prospective groom. After a brief but no doubt impressive rant, he set about renting the largest vehicle he could find, then stuffed my full-figured aunt and my tiny mother, their commodious and extensive array of brand-new matching luggage—and himself—into the rented car.

Up they drove, around hairpin turns on winding mountain roads that, if anyone leaned an inch too far in the wrong direction, would send them flying over the precipice to their doom. Finally, they reached the groom's village, where they were greeted by my father's worst nightmare. "Rustic" did not do it justice, from all that I heard for many years after. No, it would have been a step up to reach rustic. It was beyond what even Dad had envisioned: They were to be accommodated in a room over the barn, where they'd have to sleep on a straw mattress. As if that weren't enough, there was no indoor plumbing. Any trips to the loo would mean going down the steps and outside to an outhouse! They had to go to a well to get water. This was definitely *not* the Hilton.

To top it all off, the party that had been promised to celebrate the arrival of the American *familia* did not materialize. My father was furious. After a subdued dinner at the groom's family home, complete with homemade wine that most likely calmed everyone down, the guests and family went off to their assigned sleeping quarters.

Early the next morning, around sunrise, my parents were awakened by the donkey alarm. The beast's braying was loud enough to wake the whole house. The donkey was later joined by the crowing of a rooster, as if the first alarm had not been sufficient to wake living and dead. Now fully awake, to my father's further disgruntlement, he found that he was decorated, head to toe, with small red bites—apparently he and Mom weren't the only occupants of that straw bed.

Infuriated, he told my mother to pack immediately. They were not spending another night in that place. They would move to more comfortable lodgings, even if he had to drive all the way back to Rome to find them.

For the rest of the week, the adventures continued. My mother saw her first and only chicken have its neck wrung while the groom's sister carried on a casual conversation with her as if nothing had happened. My aunt and her fiancé took my parents sightseeing in Pompeii, which they enjoyed a great deal. But otherwise most of the week involved filling out forms and traveling to and from the town hall, the church, and the various authorities whose official stamps had to be affixed to all the appropriate documents before the wedding could take place.

Finally the wedding day arrived, but at the church came the next glitch. At the door of the church, when the priest spied my aunt's beautiful off-the-shoulder wedding gown with its deep décolletage, he forbade my aunt to enter *his* church! That dress was simply too revealing to be proper in a house of worship—so typical of those scandalous Americans! Without a cover-up of some kind, there was not going to be a wedding that day, at least not in *that* wedding gown.

After a great deal of commotion, begging, pleading, and tears, "donations," and no doubt other persuasive tactics, the priest relented and handed my aunt an altar cloth to drape over her shoulders. So much for sophisticated, expensive New York fashion.

Meanwhile, my father, who in his spare time aspired to be Cecil B. DeMille, was filming the ceremony—that is, until the priest noticed his movie camera. From the altar he motioned to stop filming, and once that last detail was settled, the couple were at last married.

Down the aisle, down the steps of the church, and out the antique doors went the bride and groom. "Cecil" got his last shots, and soon they were all on their way, on foot, to a local restaurant to celebrate the wedding with a feast.

Early the next morning, at the first light of dawn, before even the donkey alarm or the rooster began their auditory ritual, my father packed the car and went off with my mother, leaving the happy couple to their honeymoon without a word of farewell to anyone.

In desperate need of a vacation after all the preparations and confusion, my parents visited an old army friend of my father, an American doctor who had married an Italian woman. Then they went on to Rome, Naples, and Capri, where they stayed in the most luxurious accommodations they could find, in an effort to erase the memory of that rustic night in the mountains.

At long last, a few weeks later, my uncle and I picked them up at Idlewild Airport, now JFK, on Long Island, where we spotted them exiting customs, but only because of my mother's giant new pink Italian lampshade of a hat.

As for me, I only saw the home movie, which I vividly remember even now. My aunt was totally draped from neck to waist by a stiff white cloth as she stepped out of church—a cloth she gripped tightly under her chin, but which somehow ended up looking like part of the outfit. She was smiling and laughing, and she and her new husband looked a little startled by the sunlight after the dim candlelight of the church. Luckily Dad was behind the camera; he did not exactly approve of the match and was said to scowl through the entire week of wedding preparations. At least that wasn't caught on film!

SURVIVAL HINTS

1. If you're going to a wedding in another country, find out exactly what your accommodations will be so that you don't have unpleasant surprises.
2. If you'll be married in a foreign country whose customs you may not understand, be sure to find out what the dress code is in houses of worship to avoid controversy—or worse! This is especially important if you are being married in a faith or country that is completely unfamiliar.

3

When the Cultures
Aren't Common

Sanity Quiz

You've just gotten engaged. Okay, so there are differences between your cultures. You're a Buddhist vegetarian and your husband is a Jewish carnivore. You're worlds apart when it comes to customs, traditions, backgrounds, and now even food! How are you supposed to come up with a wedding ceremony that satisfies everyone's family and friends?

Do you
A. use two separate caterers and hope for the best
B. have two separate weddings
C. give up on the wedding and just live together—you'll figure out the food as you go
D. elope to escape the confusion

If you chose any of these answers, then you probably can use some advice. Read on and see how our delightful contributors coped!

Clash of Cultures? Hardly!

Mary Kim

MY FIANCÉ, HOWIE Kim, was Korean and I wasn't. It didn't matter to us, but it did matter to his mother and father, and during the eight years that we were together before our marriage, I had never met them because they strongly objected to the match.

Then there was another problem—our age difference. When we started to date, Howie was in his twenties while I was in my early thirties. We were about ten years apart, although I looked young for my age. But his parents weren't comfortable with this difference either.

Perhaps the other significant problem for his parents was that we were living together but we weren't getting married. At some point we had gotten engaged, and for the next seven years or so we just stayed that way.

Things began to change for us, though, when we made a cross-country trip together, from New York to the

West Coast. It was a great adventure, though our car ulti-
mately broke down in Oregon, where we got help from
some of Howie's relatives, who lived there. It was a wonderful trip and a great opportunity to really see America.

On the way back, when I saw the New York skyline, I
got tears in my eyes, because at the moment, if I had
never realized it before, I knew how much I loved Howie
and I was happy to realize that I was going to spend the
rest of my life with him.

I told him how I felt, and we started to make arrangements to get married at last. Finally, I met his parents at
dinner. His mother, Mija, was warm and open, but his father was much less so. Since I am an independent kind
of person, I truly didn't worry about it. I was marrying
Howie, not his father.

But then the differences in the cultures began to
emerge. During the time it took to plan the wedding,
Mija repeatedly lobbied for us to have two wedding ceremonies. We had planned to be married by a Native
American priest I know, but Mija asked us to be married
by a Catholic priest (not my religion)—and also to have
a separate, full-blown Korean ceremony. I wasn't sure
what a Korean ceremony entailed, but I wasn't going to
sweat it because I believe it's the best way to approach
life. I agreed to both of her requests.

As it happened, we got married at a place called
Callahan's Beach in Huntington, New York, and it cost
us nothing except for the caterer. Half of the food was
Korean and half was American fare. Music was provided

by my future father-in-law, who played the organ, and by my new sister-in-law, Charlotte, who played the violin with her husband, a music teacher who could play any instrument or song.

Half of the guests were Korean. Half were not. But it was the Korean ceremony that impressed me. After we were married by the Catholic priest, everyone donned gloriously colorful Korean costumes and we participated in a ceremony that was at once moving and beautiful. Far from being something that created conflict, it created beauty, warmth, and togetherness.

One final note: We've had our first baby, a little boy, who is—pardon my objective analysis—gorgeous. And, appropriately enough, when he's asleep he looks Caucasian, and when he's awake, those penetrating dark eyes clearly show off his Korean extraction!

My advice to anyone having a dual wedding ceremony: Don't be afraid of it—you'll enjoy it!

SURVIVAL HINTS

1. If you're planning a wedding around two cultures, it's important that both groups are included equally and feel that their heritages are being respected and celebrated.

2. Try to be open and accepting of suggestions from your fiancé's parents regarding their different cultural traditions so that the day can be special for them as well as for you.

Planning an Interfaith Wedding

Kathleen Walsh Zimmerman

PLANNING AN INTERFAITH wedding isn't as simple as you might think. Take it from me. I know. I grew up in an Irish Catholic family—a huge one. There were nine of us, and I was the second oldest. After dating all sorts of Irish and other assorted Catholic boys, whom did I meet and fall in love with in college but Ralph Zimmerman.

We're a well-matched couple. We're both short with dark hair and blue eyes, and we have the same sense of humor, values, dreams, and ideals. The only area where we don't match is religion. He's Jewish, I'm not. But we weren't worried that it would cause us trouble, and each of our families accepted the newcomer with open arms.

In fact, the initial planning of our wedding couldn't have been easier. We had no problem with the bridal party, the families, the outfits, the reception hall, the date, the menu—nothing. That is, until we went to my church, St. Margaret's, to book the wedding. The priest, who knew me and my family, welcomed Ralph and me into his office. When I told him that we wanted the wedding in the church, he was receptive. But when I asked if we could have a rabbi co-officiate, he frowned. "Hmmm. I don't think we can allow that. The archdiocese is very strict these days—a reaction to the liberal thinking of the past two decades."

"What if we didn't have a Mass, but just a wedding service?" I asked.

"Well . . . ," he began, "if you could find an agreeable rabbi, maybe we could work something out."

We left with the hope that we'd be back to book the service. Little did we know that the church had been the easy part!

Since Ralph was from Philadelphia, he hoped to ask his rabbi to handle it, but he was not available on the date that we'd booked the reception. Not only that, but it was really too much for the elderly man to have to drive three hours for the ceremony in New Jersey. Reluctantly Ralph decided to ask his local friends if they knew of a liberal rabbi. After calls to at least six referrals, Ralph was totally frustrated. Nobody would agree to co-officiate at a wedding inside a church. It just wasn't going to happen, even with Reformed rabbis, who are the most liberal rabbis in Judaism.

Sensing our gloom, my father made a suggestion. "Would the priest and the rabbi go along with a ceremony at the reception hall instead of a church? It'd be neutral territory and then they'd be on equal footing." Ralph and I agreed that this was a good alternative, and although I'd have liked to be married in my parish, I was glad to have a chance at having both faiths represented at the wedding, for our sake as well as for both families.

After calling the priest and the rabbi Ralph liked best, we were elated! Both of them agreed to participate, and they decided to confer ahead of time to work out the details of the shared ceremony at the reception hall. We were very lucky it worked out.

On the day of the wedding, with our guests waiting in the chapel of the beautiful reception hall, we all felt that both families were satisfied with the outcome. The rabbi led off the service, and the priest continued up to the exchange of vows. Then they both asked us in unison to repeat the vows. It was beautiful, and it went without a hitch. The priest gave the Catholic blessing, followed by the rabbi's in Hebrew; my husband broke the glass, we kissed, and everyone applauded.

So if you're planning an interfaith service, don't be locked into preconceived ideas. Sometimes you have to be flexible to keep everyone happy, and I know from personal experience, this was one of the most beautiful weddings I've seen, even if I'm a bit biased!

SURVIVAL HINTS

1. Sometimes neutral territory is the best place for an interfaith service so nobody feels favored or slighted.

2. Try to involve representatives of both faiths so that the traditions of each can be melded into the service. After all, the families will be merging those traditions too, and the symbolism won't be lost on the guests.

My Jewish-Italian Wedding

Anna Bodini Schwartz

I WAS A nervous wreck. It was three years ago, but it feels like last week. Here I was, an only child, and I was going to be married. My mother was deceased, and my father, grandparents, aunts, and uncles were excited and more wound up than usual for such events, and to an extent that nobody could miss. As with any wedding, there was a great deal of planning to do, but everyone kept saying it was much more complicated and different from the usual family weddings, especially because it wasn't on familiar territory. There was a reason for this.

I, who had attended the local Catholic schools all the way through high school, had gone to college and met and fallen in love with a nice Jewish boy. We were to be married, but first I'd needed to convert to Judaism, which I did without hesitation. It took a year of studying, but I enjoyed the task.

Although a few of the elderly and more religious women in the family were concerned about my immortal and formerly Catholic soul, everyone else was glad that I was doing what made me happy. My grandparents, having emigrated from Italy in their youth, were not at all concerned about the differences in our backgrounds, and they welcomed their new Jewish grandson into the family.

The wedding and reception were held at the local synagogue, a place none of my family had been inside before. There were plenty of excited children running around, both Italian and Jewish, and games were organized by the brigade of mothers to keep them busy.

The ceremony itself was traditional and in Hebrew. I'd rehearsed my part for months, had been unbelievably worried about screwing up my lines, but it all went perfectly. The cantor's voice was especially beautiful that day, and at the end of the marriage service, my husband broke the glass, everyone shouted *mazel tov,* even the Italians, and then we all moved from the chapel to the banquet room.

As with most Italian weddings, there was lively music and, of course, plenty of food. If any two groups shared common ground on something, for Italians and Jews it's the quality and quantity of the food that's served at any event, public or private. There the two cultures fit like puzzle pieces. And luckily for me, there was a local Italian-Jewish caterer in town.

Probably the funniest sight of all was watching my Italian grandfather and uncles all in yarmulkes trying to dance the hora. Somehow it kept turning into the tarantella (I guess old habits die hard). But everyone had fun, and we all danced until the sun was almost up. Eventually the Italians began singing opera arias, especially my grandfather and great-uncle, and a great time was had by all.

Our Italian-Jewish wedding had a great beginning, and our extended blended family has now increased by two. Now *that* is a cause for celebration, and that Italian-Jewish caterer really loves our combined clan!

SURVIVAL HINTS

1. If you're marrying someone outside your faith and decide to convert, don't get talked out of it by anyone. It's your decision and faith is a personal matter.
2. If you're combining two diverse cultures, it's great if you can find common ground, especially if it involves food, music, or children.

Between Friends

H. A. Feldman

THIS IS THE story of my grandparents, my father's parents, who made the best of a difficult situation, raised a large family in the United States during the Great Depression, and stayed married and true to each other their entire lives. I don't think they ever had a formal wedding.

Hinde was eighteen, Feiwel was seventeen. They were friendly and lived in neighboring Russian towns of Libozin and Degitzin on the Polish-Russian border. They decided to leave Russia for the United States because it wasn't safe for Jews to live in Russia as the pogroms became more common. But getting out of there in the early 1900s was difficult. Although they were only acquaintances, they had heard that it was easier for married couples to obtain the required travel visas and permits, so they married quietly and privately. It was never expected or intended to be a lifelong commitment.

In late winter of 1912, they somehow made their way to Antwerp, Belgium, where they boarded the charter passenger ship *Vaderland*, bound for Ellis Island, New York. The ship was built in Scotland in 1900 and carried 1,162 passengers. Feiwel traveled in second-class accommodations, and Hinde was in steerage, or third class. He was able to share his meager food ration with her during the trip by smuggling it to her below deck. They were both seasick much of the time.

On March 14, 1912, the SS *Vaderland* arrived in New York. For Russian peasants who had never been on a boat before, the ocean travel in the winter must have been quite an ordeal. They were processed by the immigration authority on Ellis Island, where they were asked their names and other information. Deciding that the pretense of being married was no longer necessary, they declared their marital status as single to the authorities, as was reflected on their respective passenger records. The passenger records also show that they modified their ages as well, both declaring they were twenty.

Feiwel's last name must have been something in Russian that was both unpronounceable and incomprehensible to the immigration clerk, who asked him his profession. He made it known somehow that he was a farmer or field hand, so his name became "Feldmann" (a German translation, from which we conclude that the clerk didn't know Russian from German).

Hinde's name, as shown on her Russian papers, was "Warshowicki," which became modified to "Worzowski" on her passenger record. Their first names, shown as "Feiwel" and "Hinde" later became Americanized as Phillip and Anna.

After clearing immigration, they went their separate ways, he to a cousin in Brooklyn, New York, and she to a cousin living in Newark, New Jersey. During his first week as a New Yorker, Phillip recounted the story of how he had managed to escape from Russia and arrive in the United States by "getting married" in Russia. His cousin was aghast. "You have a wife in New Jersey?" he shouted. "You can't live with us. You should be living with her!"

Having been kicked out by his cousin, Phillip set off for Newark to find his friend Hinde, with whom he eventually reconnected.

Although they never officially married in America, they stayed together for the rest of their lives, and raised eight children. Their first son, Nathan, born in 1913, was my father. When Anna died in 1987, she was the grandmother of twenty, great-grandmother of twenty-one, and had one great-great-granddaughter. Nathan is now age ninety-three and still going strong.

The Mixed (Up) Marriage

Ginny Chandoha

I WAS RAISED Methodist, but that never stopped me from embracing people of all faiths. I count among my many diverse friends Christians, Jews, Buddhists, and Muslims. I have learned many philosophies, and my adult beliefs aren't part of an organized faith at all. Rather, I believe that we are all human beings, that there is a reason for everything, even if that reason isn't always revealed to us right away; eventually it will be clear. When one door closes, another opens. There are always signs, if we can recognize and interpret them, and we will be shown the path to take. Even if something we perceive as bad happens, it is for a reason, and brings us to the place where we are supposed to be.

I was very young when I met an older man of Jewish faith. I thought I was in love with him, and agreed to marry him. My parents were thrilled that their only daughter had found a husband, and his parents were thrilled that he had found a wife. Both sets of parents set aside their religious differences. Or so I thought.

As the wedding date drew nearer, the objections grew louder. My mother insisted that the wedding take place in the church, while his parents were against it. Caught in between, I attempted to appease both sides. I suggested we have both a rabbi and a minister officiate the ceremony. That was OK with my mom, but it was objectionable to my future mother-in-law because it would still be held in a church.

All right. What if we had back-to-back ceremonies? How about we marry in a synagogue to satisfy my husband's family, and then have a church wedding for my parents? Well, that suggestion didn't work either. My mother made it very plain to me that if I wasn't married in a church first, there would be no church wedding at all. Okay. And the reverse sequence wouldn't work for my future in-laws either.

This quandary went on for weeks, and I no longer had to worry about fitting into my wedding gown. I was so beside myself with trying to make everyone else happy that I no longer had any appetite. I also began having doubts about marrying at all. If it was so much hassle now, what would the future hold? I refused to listen to that tiny inner voice, and continued with the mental gyrations to resolve the wedding day blues.

Finally I devised a plan that made everyone happy except me. I married my husband in a secret ceremony, with only his parents and a handful of his friends in attendance, never breathing a word of it to my friends or to my family. Six months later I walked down the aisle of the church, with my proud parents and all of their friends and family in attendance.

My mother whispered in my ear, as I was about to walk down the aisle, that she hoped I would be happy. I distinctly remember crying. Not because it was the happiest day of my life, but because I knew that what I was doing was a sham. And I already knew that my marriage was coming apart at the seams. I went through with the charade, but only a few months later filed for divorce.

Feeling despondent, I took up photography while I awaited my divorce ruling. One day I walked into the camera shop I had been frequenting, only to discover a new guy working behind the counter. He turned out to be the love of my life.

SURVIVAL HINTS

1. If you have any doubts about your relationship, before you marry is the time to face them.
2. If your family or friends have doubts about your upcoming marriage, listen to them—but then make up your own mind.
3. If you decide it's the wrong move, better to call it off, even the day of the wedding, rather than do something that isn't right for you.

4

When the Wedding Party Is Disorderly...Or a Bit Different

Wedding Wows
Wanda Lauerman

The Bachelor Party
Jan Mulineau

The Flower Dog
Jessie Ellis

No Need to Be Included
Samantha Hernandez

Homespun Brides
Lee Goldstein

Picking My Perfect Bridesmaids
Helen Heidelmeir

Thank Heaven for Best Friends
Sherry Lee

Sanity Quiz

Your best man shows up in his tuxedo wearing a nose ring and a bandana wrapped around his head. Now these distinctive items are his trademarks, and he's been wearing the bandana ever since you have known him. But you thought your wedding would be the exception.

Do you
A. ask him kindly to remove it and the nose ring or you'll choke him with the bandana
B. have the rest of the wedding party add a bandana to their ensemble
C. ignore it—someone else can deal with him
D. quickly call for a stand-in

No matter how you answered this question, you'll sympathize with our contributors who had their own wedding party problems.

Wedding Wows

Wanda Lauerman

I NEVER THOUGHT I would get married. From my personal family experience, no one was happily married. So whatever would make me do such a thing as not only get married but also have a big elaborate wedding? Marriage hardly made the top ten list of things for a woman to aspire to. But I loved my husband from the first moment I saw him. By the time we had been living together for four years, he had already been asking "the question" for at least two. I always replied: "You can't just ask. You need a ring or something, don't you?"

So, one day he came home, starving as usual, stuffed his mouth full of saltines and in a no-nonsense kind of tone asked, "Do you love me?"

I said, "Yes."

"Do you want to marry me?"

I said "Yes, but . . . "

He said, "OK," and told me he had a jeweler lined up with a fabulous gem for a good price, and that we could see it at a mall somewhere soon. His part in the business of planning our wedding was now apparently complete. As I took over, I heard nary an objection from him on the subject.

I spent the next several months leafing through bridal magazines, so obsessed with the dress that my dog and cat sat at my feet with worried expressions over the constant turning of pages of multiple volumes. That was my part in the insanity, aside from visiting every bridal shop in New Jersey, even to the point of being forty miles south of home, losing the brakes on my Volkswagen, and having to be towed all the way back from a nothing-out-of-the-ordinary bridal selection in godforsaken Middletown. I also was jarred back to reality one day at an ATM machine when I discovered that my personal bank account was overdrawn; I had been so busy with finding *the dress* that I had hardly paid any attention to my finances.

I also loved my best girlfriend since the moment I saw her. And, as most anyone who knows her realizes, this wonderful free spirit was, and still is, living life according to her own rules. Now try to imagine shopping in Manhattan with someone who you aren't sure has a Social Security number, and trying to put together the ceremonial headdresses of the maid of honor (guess who) and bridesmaids with such a free spirit. She disappeared while we were in the fashion district. I walked out of a shop and up the street to find that she had developed a recent "thing" for hot dogs and left me for street meat. Just prior to the wedding, this best friend and maid of honor of mine had made plans to move upstate. On the night before her move, she went out on the town to celebrate, but just as she arrived home that night, she was assaulted by a mugger, who broke her cheekbone. She ended up in the hospital and in need of major facial reconstruction.

Along with my free-spirited best friend, I had asked my cousins in Los Angeles to be bridesmaids. One of them said, "You're not going to have all that chiffon, are you?" She agreed to be an attendant if she could tolerate the dress. I tried not to let that bother me. My other cousin agreed to participate, but having an aversion to flying, she took the train across the whole blessed country. She stepped off the train at a stop somewhere, leaving her purse on board, and had her wallet stolen. She arrived in need of a loan. Did I mention that I loved both my cousins from the moment they were born? I have yet another beloved cousin who agreed to be a bridesmaid on the spot. For a short period of time, she even honored my request to stand in for the wounded maid of honor.

But still I was wrestling with the fact that my best friend was spending her days and nights in headgear that resembled a gyroscope. Just before the wedding, I visited her while she recuperated at her sister's home, and we decided that she was hardly in any condition to be in a wedding party. But after leaving her, I grew uneasy with my decision to replace her. She was my best friend, after all, and she really looked only a little swollen and teary (other than the gyroscope). No matter how she looked, she should be my maid of honor. I called her to tell her, and we agreed that was what we both really wanted.

On my wedding day, one of my cousins from Los Angeles learned of my maid of honor's rather startling looking condition and hesitated to stand next to her. Thankfully, my other bridesmaid traded places without drama.

My wedding dress turned out fine, despite the train my mother had insisted on. But I won out on the short veil instead of whatever else might have ended up on my head, if my mom had had her say.

My parents gave us a wonderful wedding reception with over a hundred guests. I'm not sure how many of my bridal attendants actually smoked back then, but by the time we were through with dinner (after a cocktail reception replete with string quartet and hot and cold hors d'oeuvres), all of the *mesdames*, bedecked in dusty rose, off-the-shoulder satin gowns, were chumming it up, waving Newports around in the air like Betty Davis. God bless champagne! Any previous reserve, whether it was over my maid of honor's condition or anything else, was now cast to the wind.

And at the end of the party, I felt like Cinderella, after receiving all those tantalizing envelopes, and the ballroom had turned back into a pumpkin. The help, being anxious to close up, had taken the tables down to their bare unmatched tops, and the room looked more like a bingo hall than a wedding reception ballroom. But the maître d' came all the way outside just to tell me that I was the most gracious bride he had ever met. I was very surprised. (Me?) Even the photos came out okay, as my maid of honor had a "good side," in spite of the photographer's insistence that I cut her out of my photo album! After all that had happened leading up to the wedding, I didn't think so!

As I reflect, I can now answer my own question, Why would I ever want a big fancy wedding? As it turns out, I did it for many reasons that experience revealed in its own good time. And, if I learned any lesson at all from planning the wedding, I believe I also did it for what still lies ahead in my married life. I believe we did it for love, and for a lifetime. We knew that a wedding would bring happiness to our parents, who, in spite of having what seemed to be bumpy relationships, had the wisdom to see us as incomplete without each other. We learned that one can actually propagate love with the birth of a child, one who instantly became the world's greatest son, grandchild, nephew, and cousin. I believe that the more surprises you experience as you plan your wedding and live as husband and wife, the more charmed your lives will seem later on when you look back on it all.

SURVIVAL HINTS

1. Before, during, and after planning your wedding, be kind and tolerant, no matter what happens.
2. Don't forget that it is your fiancé's wedding, too, so include him in the planning.
3. Try to do most of your screaming when you're alone.
4. Let go a little and let the magic happen on its own.
5. Remember that a wedding is just a beautiful day, but a marriage is for a lifetime.

The Bachelor Party

Jan Mulineau

HONESTLY, THE LAST thing I wanted was my husband-to-be and his drunken buddies out watching some stripper strut her unclothed stuff. I could imagine it over and over again: His best buddy, who I didn't like all that much to begin with, offering up cash for my honey's last lap dance.

It was a tug-of-war between us all along: The best friend and the newfound love. Who would win the prize? His best friend, still single and girlfriendless at the time, probably would have bet on himself, but was he ever wrong. New love conquers all. It can even stomp out the best of friendships, at least temporarily.

I didn't want to end their friendship, but I also didn't want my fiancé's best friend to cause all the trouble he possibly could to regain his friend and cost me what was now the most important relationship in my life. After all, this was the love of my life we are talking about, the man I was about to marry.

I found the best solution to the dreaded bachelor party was to put the situation in the hands of my heart-less girlfriends . . . the females in the wedding party. The more the men talked about the bachelor party, the more the ladies filled my future husband's head with details of how the final *single* girls night out would be.

My bridesmaid Shelly, the most boisterous of the bunch, left absolutely nothing to my fiancé's imagina-tion. She went on and on while the other girls threw in their tidbits of emphasis. But Shelly had this way of exag-gerating. When she began describing the wild night we would have, only one male stripper was involved. By the time she was done, we had a private room booked at a swanky hotel and there was not one but five guys taking it all off. One for each of us in the wedding party . . . in-cluding me!

If there is anything you can count on in life it's jeal-ousy in a man. That green-eyed monster will show itself repeatedly throughout the course of your marriage. There is really nothing you can do about it other than to use it to your advantage. I certainly did.

This earthy description of raw, naked, sex-ridden be-havior at the upcoming bachelorette party poured out as Shelly continued to fill my intended's brain. This soon put an end to his desire to have any sort of a bachelor party! I remember the night he came to me, full of all the nonsense Shelly had fed him. It went something like this:

"Honey, I don't think I want to have a bachelor party. It really makes no sense to go out and get drunk the night before our big day so we can feel like crap all day long at our wedding." (Notice the word *we*.)

Now, not to let him off too easily, I replied: "Well, we don't have to do it the night before. We can do it the weekend before. That way we will all be recovered from any hangovers and no one will look like the walking dead on the big day."

He didn't know what to say at this point, but he clearly wanted to opt out. But I wasn't giving in that easily because before Shelly fed him the line he was all gung ho. He must have thought we were going to have a tea party while he was out watching some stripper shake it for him. I stood my ground.

"Look," I said, "they really want to take us out. It's important to them."

Then he finally broke down and told me the truth. He didn't want the girls doing for me what the guys had planned for him. I told him he could forget about me allowing him that wild experience if it wasn't extended to me as well. It took him about two minutes to come up with a solution:

"How about we all go out together, the whole wedding party," he said.

"What a great idea!" I replied.

SURVIVAL HINTS

1. If you're concerned about an out-of-control bachelor party, speak up. Better that than resentment later.

2. Consider alternative forms of celebrations for the bride and groom, including the entire wedding party or individual nights out for bride and groom. Plans could include going to the theater, a bowling party, ice- or roller-skating, playing basketball or softball—whatever activity the guest of honor enjoys that doesn't involve witnessing or participating in lewd behavior for either group.

The Flower Dog

Jessie Ellis

SOME WEDDINGS ARE just a little offbeat. Sometimes the guests are a bit—how shall I put this—different. In other cases, it's the wedding party that sets things off from the ordinary. But for this particular wedding, it was two of the members of the bridal party who made this such a distinctive event—and partly because of their behavior. I can't say it's never happened before, but this was a first of its kind for me, as mother of the bride.

It was a beautiful summer's day. Perfect for our little girl's unconventional nuptials. She got married on the spur of the moment with only two days' notice. A day before the wedding, I went to an art show to view a Buddhist sand painting in progress by a visiting monk from Mongolia. There I got a saffron scarf for her wedding, which was blessed by the monk.

The next day was beautiful. The friendly outdoor wedding had its charms: an airy, wooded scene, a bride and groom who would discuss their matching tattoos, and the flower dog and ring-bearer dog—a brother and sister duo with matching decorated collars. All of the guests liked the eccentricity of it all.

The ceremony proceeded as planned. The bride looked lovely in her one-of-a-kind exotic wedding dress as she walked down the aisle escorted by myself and her father. The groom beamed at the front. The flower dog and ring-bearer dog trotted amiably down the aisle, sniffing some guests, and stealthily licking the sandaled toes of others.

But dogs don't understand about being serious. They are oblivious to solemn events and, frankly, dogs will be dogs. During the ceremony the ring bearer bit at a flea and licked himself inappropriately. But that was nothing compared to what followed.

As the happy couple paused to exchange their vows, the flower dog, not to be outdone by her partner, began to "hork." Not a dainty little gag, but rather a booming, disgusting, *Hoooorrrkkk! Hooorkkk!*

Everyone giggled, nervously. The flower dog licked her chops, and the ceremony went on as scheduled.

Nobody thought twice as the human and canine couples greeted the wedding guests and then proceeded to the reception. At the dinner after the wedding, the bride immediately tied my blessed saffron scarf around her neck like the free spirit that she is. The truth is *she* is the blessing. And nobody stood too close when the flower dog enjoyed her own piece of wedding cake!

SURVIVAL HINTS

1. When including nonhumans in your wedding party, be prepared for nonstandard behavior.
2. If you decide to include animals, be sure to walk them first and don't feed them too close to the ceremony!

No Need to Be Included

Samantha Hernandez

WHY IS IT people always feel the need to include everyone and anyone they know in their wedding party? I was asked by my brother-in-law's fiancée if I would be a bridesmaid in her party. Now that's all well and good, and I agreed, not because I wanted to be in the wedding, but rather because I thought they needed me. They had an unpaired groomsman, so to even out the wedding party, they needed me as an extra—or so I thought!

You may ask why I would think such a thing. Well, first off, I had met the bride-to-be only once before, and our total conversation on that day lasted maybe ten minutes, five of which were spent asking me to be in her wedding. I don't know about you, but at that point I still considered myself a stranger, and normally you don't go around asking strangers to be in your wedding party.

My second thought was maybe she just doesn't have many friends; she is stuck in a situation and needs help. Okay, I'll help her out, but not before making sure that on some crazy level she wasn't doing this for my benefit. You see, my husband, the brother of the groom, was going to be the best man. Our initial conversation went something like this:

FUTURE SISTER-IN-LAW: "Hi, I'm Linda."
BROTHER-IN-LAW: "Oops, I forgot to introduce you."
ME: "Hi, have a seat."
BROTHER-IN-LAW: "Freezing out today."
FUTURE SISTER-IN-LAW: "Sure is."
ME: "Yes, I'm looking forward to warmer weather."

My brother-in-law at this point slinked out of the room so he was not involved in the hit. After we sat in complete silence for a few long moments, she got to the point.

FUTURE SISTER-IN-LAW: "So, I wanted to ask you: Can you be a bridesmaid for us?"

Steadying myself on the chair so I didn't fall off, I was dumbfounded. My thoughts were, Are you crazy? I don't even know you. Am I dreaming? Is this *Candid Camera*?

Realizing she was intently waiting for my answer, I reluctantly agreed, but not before saying:

ME: "Well, yeah, I can do it for you. But if you are asking because you think I need to be included for some reason, don't feel obligated. I don't feel the need to be included at all, so please don't ask me if that is your reasoning, because I am quite fine just sitting on the sidelines."

FUTURE SISTER-IN-LAW (in another awkward moment): "Oh no. We really want you to be in it. Can you do it?"

I agreed with immediate regret, because now I had been placed in an awkward situation where I didn't want to hurt anyone's feelings, but I also really didn't want to take part.

Then I began to wonder if this was my brother-in-law's idea. Was he the one with the need to include everyone? Was he the one making this awkward moment even more awkward? I really can't imagine what would make someone ask a complete stranger to be in her wedding. In my opinion, a wedding party is supposed to be made up of those nearest and dearest to you, not someone you just met. Hell, if that's the case, you'd be better off hiring a bunch of models to do it. At least the pictures would be beautiful!

I've only seen Linda once since that day, and that was for a dress fitting. I think maybe we said two words to each other. I'm still trying to find a way *out*. I'm hoping for a broken leg, a bad case of chicken pox, or some other contagious disease or disaster that will keep me far from the wedding party and somewhat sane.

SURVIVAL HINTS

1. Not everyone feels the need to be included in your wedding, so choose your wedding party carefully. Try to include only those people you really want.
2. Most people won't say no to avoid hurt feelings, so try not to put them on the spot if you have any doubt that they'd want to participate.

Homespun Brides

Lee Goldstein

I'VE NEVER FORGOTTEN being a bridesmaid for my college roommate, Melanie. We'd both been art students at Pratt Institute, in Brooklyn. Melanie and I didn't talk religion, but I knew she was a Baptist, and took her religion seriously. On Sunday mornings, she'd actually get up early and go to church. There were three of us in the room, and aside from Melanie, our idea of religion then was a food exchange. I brought the bagels; Melanie made johnnycakes and hush puppies, exotic names for fried starch.

Melanie and Matt, her childhood sweetheart, became engaged and the wedding was planned to be in her hometown. Melanie's mom couldn't understand why Melanie would want the wedding to be anywhere but behind the firehouse, but Melanie insisted she didn't want it to be on blacktop. The wedding would be in her parents' backyard.

Tradition had it that the entire congregation was invited. Melanie's mom got promises for picnic tables and the plans were begun.

I was one of four bridesmaids; three of us were from Pratt. We were told to arrive at Melanie's house two days before the wedding. I hadn't seen Melanie since graduation a month before; she'd been busy sewing her dress!

The first order of business was to decorate straw bonnets, which Mom placed before us. Her mom was a pack rat, she had shoe boxes full of ribbons, beads, buttons, charms, bows, and thread, and we dug in. This might have been a dangerous idea; we were art students and this was the 1960s. The bonnets might have come out looking like they were from Haight-Ashbury. Maybe they did. I do remember weird things going up off the bonnets and a "who has the tallest bonnet" contest. Mom didn't have a color scheme for us, or a theme—we just dug in.

The day before the wedding, Mom brought in the food. Not prepared food, mind you, but food that we all would make and assemble. I was on bologna and ham detail, rolling up thousands of round pieces and spearing them with toothpicks. Mom made coleslaw in the sink. God knows what was going on in the bathtub.

The wedding, Melanie had told us, would be full of restrictions. No music. No liquor. No dancing. She was worried that we would think it boring, but, for me, it was wonderful and I proudly wore my bonnet perched on my head.

Many years later, when my own daughter, Emily, and I planned her wedding, I insisted we bring in some of Melanie's wedding-planning strategies. Despite reservations, my daughter, a rational lawyer, gave in to my plan to have the bridesmaids make their own bouquets. It'll be fun, I said, and simple—not like making bonnets. I'll get an assortment of flowers. I'll get ribbons, wires, fabric. We'll bond.

Emily googled instructions on how to make wedding bouquets, but I wanted none of that. No directions, just creativity. Emily thought we'd be cutting it close—one of the bridesmaids was flying in the day before the wedding. No problem, we'll make hers too. I bought wine (white, of course, lest it drip on the flowers), and plenty of food for decorating day.

The girls came at two, the day before the wedding. I had everything laid out on a table, just like Melanie's mom. The girls took flowers, counting them to make sure they had the same number in each bouquet, discussed arrangements, decided on a theme, and went to work. In a half an hour, the bouquets were finished, and they were all identical. That was fun, they said. What's next? Next? Nothing. Nothing? Oh. Well, let's go out for a drink, they said, and left quite happy.

I spent the next hour cleaning up, listening to the Jefferson Airplane, thinking of Melanie. You really can't go home after all.

Picking My Perfect Bridesmaids

Helen Heidelmeir

THINK OF A bride as a wedding CEO. Besides being the guest of honor and center of attention, being the bride-to-be requires skills in bridesmaid selection and survival. As creative director of your own wedding, your job can be pleasant if you know what to do and how to do it. Like all brides, I had to be a creative bridesmaid recruiter, and you can do it too. I had to choose among twenty cousins and scores of friends. What did I do? I picked the most reliable—and steady—ones in the bunch.

In early Roman times, bridesmaids formed a protective screen around the bride as they led her to the groom's village. These human shields were there to ward off any hooligans or undesirable suitors. Think about your girlfriends and which ones could fill this kind of a role? I picked two who liked to ride motorcycles for a hobby as my personal nuptial phalanx. Despite the image the motorcycles may bring to mind, my bridesmaids are also lovely and graceful women.

Today's bridesmaid's role has evolved into that of supporter, assistant, and confidant to the bride. Her main function is to be the bride's "I'll be there for you when you can't take it anymore" adviser. Did I mention that my motorcycling maids are also social workers? It's true. They are both therapists at the local hospital, and those skills sure came in handy when my brother inexplicably opted out of the wedding party! They found him, sat him down, had an unofficial dual therapy session, and soon he was back in the saddle, so to speak. Whatever they said worked—it's handy having therapists on staff at a wedding!

Choosing your bridal party, of course, is a major decision. Choosing the wrong attendant, one whom you don't totally trust to be there for you during this hectic time, is not wise. This is no time to pick a casual friend or someone going through the motions just as a favor. Instead, make your selections from among lifelong friends and close family members. Going with your inner circle is your best insurance against trouble and will simplify matters because you know each other well. Did I mention that one of these social workers is my second cousin, and the other I've known since kindergarten?

They know every guy I've dated, and if I can't trust them to watch out for me, then who can I trust?

Having your nearest and dearest as attendants doesn't guarantee your wedding will go smoothly, but it will help in case things go wrong. And with these cronies surrounding you, there's a better chance that more things will go right. Still, you may want to spell out your expectations up front so that there are no misunderstandings with your bridal team along the way. You need your "staff" to be there for you—all the time—no matter how uptight you are. They also should know that with their honored position comes responsibility. You don't want to be worrying that they'd back out of the wedding party at the last minute, and if you are careful with your selection, it will never happen.

Since my squad knew me so well, they understood instinctively when I needed to be left alone or when I needed them to take charge, such as with that vicious aunt-in-law to be! It's part of the role of bridesmaid to run interference as much as possible.

Sometimes you may feel awkward when making demands on your "team." But playing it straight from the start can help you avoid trouble later, in case some well-meaning bridesmaids offer unsolicited opinions on improving your wedding plans. Although it may be tough at times to keep your cool during the planning stage, try not to get impatient with your team and recognize that their suggestions are meant to help you. My bridesmaids, for instance, had the patience of saints: They knew how to keep me calm, such as when my niece stepped on my veil. They'd already been doing it for years!

Remember, you are surrounding yourself with the people who care about you and it's their job to help you. That's the beauty of being encircled and protected by your loved ones, just like in Roman times. With my motorcycling social workers surrounding me on my wedding day, I hadn't a care in the world.

If you pick your bridesmaids well, you'll soon be focused happily on only one thing—celebrating the big event. That's the only important thing you should have to think about on your wedding day, a day when you're legitimately and happily the center of attention. Enjoy it!

SURVIVAL HINTS

1. Remember, it is of the utmost importance to continue to nurture the friendships you had before your marriage. You will never know when you may truly need your friends again.

2. Don't forget that sometimes making even the smallest effort, like a simple, "Thanks for being there," can make all the difference to your devoted friends and family.

Thank Heaven for Best Friends

Sherry Lee

THIS IS THE STORY of my disrupted wedding party. Shortly after I got engaged, I chose my wedding party with the greatest of care. I selected my closest friends and family to participate in and share my day. But what I didn't know was that during this selection process, I was in for a huge surprise.

My best friend, Deb, had just given birth by cesarean delivery to an adorable little boy, and unfortunately could not be in the wedding as a result. But I still had three of my closest friends as bridesmaids and I was okay with that. Luckily, Deb was still planning to come to the wedding, but wasn't up for being a bridesmaid so soon after giving birth.

We had a week and a half to go before the big day when my phone rang. It was my bridesmaid Stacy's brother. He sounded worried and was calling with an apology on behalf of his sister. To my shock, Stacy had admitted herself to a rehabilitation center for drug addiction. She would be living there during the three-month program, and unfortunately would not even be able to attend the wedding, let alone take part as a bridesmaid. At first I was confused; I didn't even know she had a problem. How could I have missed something like that since we were so close? I was beside myself with worry about her, and hoped she would be okay. After sending my love via her brother, I hung up the phone.

But soon I panicked when I remembered Stacy was an important member of my bridal party. Her absence would be a problem because we didn't want an unmatched groomsman, but that's what we had now that Stacy was out. How was I going to get a replacement bridesmaid with only a week and a half's notice?

Even if I could find someone to replace Stacy, how were we going to have another dress ordered and tailored with so little time left? The answer was no way. I gave up hope of solving the problem. That is, until I called Deb. She was still slightly under the influence of painkillers from her cesarean delivery, but she agreed to do her best to help me out. I gave a sigh of relief, but I still wasn't sure we were going to pull off this bridesmaid switch.

After calling the seamstress at the bridal shop and also discussing the situation with Stacy's family, we decided to try to squeeze a postdelivery Deb into skinny-mini Stacy's dress. We were working with at least a three-size difference between them, and there was no way to make a small dress bigger without additional fabric. The seamstress said she could rush order the extra fabric, and although there was no time to spare, she thought she could swing it. And sure enough, somehow she made our wedding deadline.

The dress was ready two full days before the big event. Too bad we never thought about the tiny matching dyed shoes. Poor Deb had to squeeze her size 8s into size 7s for the whole day. Thank heaven for best friends!

SURVIVAL HINTS

1. Be prepared for anything when you're planning a wedding because trouble can be waiting in the wings.
2. Always look for help from the people closest to you. They usually are more willing to go the extra mile to help you, regardless of their own situations.
3. Make sure you remind yourself once in a while how lucky you are to have close friends, and especially a best friend. It's a good idea to tell them so, too.

5

And Not Becoming a Beastly Bride

Sanity Quiz

You used to be so good-humored, up until you started planning this wedding, that is. Now every time someone mentions your name it's no longer just Susie. Instead they're calling you Her Ladyship Susie Who Bitches-a-lot. Even though they deny it, you've heard them talking behind your back. You don't understand why everyone is being so mean.

Do you
A. stand back and take a good look at yourself
B. ask your nearest and dearest what is wrong with you
C. agree you've been a bit demanding but it's just because you want your wedding to be perfect
D. apologize to those you have scared and try to be more pleasant
E. elope

If you've answered yes to any of these questions, you need to read on and find out what happened to our stalwart writers!

Dealing with Bridezilla

Juanita Jacobsen

I'M A FLORIST by profession and one of my specialties is weddings. About half of my business comes from these happy events. Over the years, I've dealt with the best of brides and the worst. The ones who want everything for nothing, and the ones who appreciate everything you do. The spoiled rotten ones, God's gift to the Earth types, and some who are very sweet.

But the one I remember most in my thirty-five-year career is the one we called "Princess Pain-in-the-Ass." That was what my staff came up with after our third bout with her. Just the sight of her pulling into the parking lot would send them all running for the back room. She was a troublemaker and no matter what you did to satisfy her, she was never happy.

Her mother came along with her on her many trips to the shop. She was a rather timid woman, and I can't imagine how she spawned this monster. Mother would sit quietly in the corner as the princess made her unreasonable demands of us all. She wanted her gardenias fresh the day of her wedding. Not fresh delivered to her, but fresh delivered to my shop. She wanted us to arrange her flowers the morning of the wedding and that morning only, to preserve their freshness longer. This brat really expected to have the red carpet rolled out for her.

But the day that took the cake was when she brought her little poodle with her into the shop. We have a No Pets policy and there is a large sign on the door that clearly states it. She strolled in carrying FiFi, with her mother following along behind, plopped the dog on the floor and started spouting demands.

I asked her to please remove FiFi from the premises. She totally ignored me and continued to make her wishes known. Next thing I knew, FiFi had made pee pee on my showroom floor, and was now running back and forth through it like a maniac, spreading it all about the room.

This was my final straw. This princess had tortured my employees and me one time too many. I lost it. I told her to take her dog and herself and kindly leave my shop, and that I wouldn't be arranging any flowers for her and God help the man who was marrying her. Then I opened the door to show her out. Princess Pain-in-the-Ass's only response was a huff, followed by an "I never!" before storming out the door. Her mother remained for a moment before getting up to leave. I noticed a smile on her face. On her way out the door, she turned to look back at me, and said, "Thank you! Thank you very much."

SURVIVAL HINTS

1. When working with professionals as you make your wedding arrangements, be reasonable. Being overly demanding won't get you anywhere, and remember that you need these people to help you make your special day the best it can be.
2. Step back and take an honest look at yourself once in a while, and remember to put yourself in the other person's place so that you only treat them as you'd want to be treated yourself.

The Bossy Bride

Jacey Kalvitz

WHEN MY BEST friend Linda asked me to be her maid of honor, I was overjoyed. It was a first for me—and I had just gotten engaged myself, so I was in the mood for weddings, in the mood for love.

However, the person I had known for over twenty years, my best friend and confidant, the person with whom I shared so many memories, began to turn from Dr. Jekyll into Ms. Hyde. She was no longer the Linda that I knew. She was more like a bad boss—bossing around all her bridesmaids, making unreasonable demands, and expecting us to drop our own lives at a second's notice and do whatever she was asking of us. She turned from kind, friendly, and funny Linda into bitchy, bossy, and downright nasty Linda. It was horrible.

One night, after a fitting for the bridesmaid gowns, for which we were all laying out our hard-earned cash, the bridesmaids, minus "bossy pants," went out for pizza. During dinner, I forget who struck the first blow, but each of us took a turn. Everyone in the party had stories to tell about Linda's outrageous demands. We all came to the conclusion that something had to be done. We loved her and wanted our real friend back, not this disturbed version of the unknown. We further agreed that someone had to talk to Linda about her behavior. Unfortunately, being the maid of honor almost automatically qualified me for this job. After attempting to get myself off the hook, I gave in and said I'd do it.

At first I didn't know how to approach the problem, but then came to the realization that straightforward is always the best approach. I asked Linda to go out for a drink after work and she agreed. I broached the subject with as much caution as I possibly could muster. I told Linda that the girls and I had been talking, and we felt that she was being a bit pushy and unreasonable with her demands.

Considering Linda's behavior for the last few weeks, I would have never expected her startling reaction: She broke down crying! She said this wedding was driving her nuts and she just couldn't take it anymore. I didn't know what to say. I hadn't realized that her bossiness was stemming from the overload she had taken on for the event. I felt terrible. Linda went on to tell me she was receiving no help from her family and that she just wanted to get it over with. She told me she never knew how difficult planning an event like this could be.

I told Linda not to worry. We'd all be happy to help.

That night we made a list of all the things Linda had to get accomplished, and the next week each one of the bridesmaids signed up to help her complete a specific task. Linda turned back into the friend we all loved and the wedding turned out fabulously in the end. After all, what are friends for?

SURVIVAL HINTS

1. Planning a wedding can be stressful, so try not to take on too much.
2. Don't be afraid to ask friends and family to help you out. Most of them will be happy to participate and are just waiting to be asked.
3. Don't let yourself get so worked up over all the things you have to do that you make it unpleasant for everyone else. It's supposed to be a happy time for everyone.

The Wedding from Hell

Judy Caruso

A FEW YEARS ago, all my friends seemed to be getting married. And somehow I ended up in 99 percent of their weddings, often as maid of honor. Most of the time I was happy to be involved because these were my closest friends' happiest occasions and it was a joy to help out. But there was this one wedding . . . .

I was working in a large company with a large number of young people who all socialized together. An ad agency, it had plenty of artists, editors, copywriters, and various other creative types who were fun to be with and with whom I had a lot in common. But one of our legion was a spoiled rich girl whose daddy had a lot of money. She also had a low-level management job at which she did not excel, mostly because she was wedding obsessed and spent all her time planning the event.

We were friendly, and she asked me to be in the wedding party. I didn't want to say yes because one of my best friends was getting married a few months later and needed my help with the planning. I didn't want to take time away from her. But I also realized that I needed to work with this woman, and if I didn't cooperate and do what she wanted, my life at work would be much more difficult. Alas, I relented and accepted the "job," and believe me, I use the term intentionally.

As might be predicted in such situations, my responsibilities with the prima donna's wedding grew and grew, kind of like a bad rash. At first all I had to do was be a bridesmaid, which under the best of circumstances with someone you aren't close to only involves trying on and paying for dresses you hate and putting up with bridal shower arrangements and expenses, most of which is orchestrated by the maid of honor and the bride's relatives, even though that's not what Emily Post dictates.

However, in the wedding from hell, there was also the maid of honor from hell. What a surprise! She, too, was a prima donna. She disappeared from the scene almost the moment the engagement ring was on the prospective bride's finger. I'm not sure if her disappearance had to do with competition, depression, or just a lack of consideration, but she was never around, couldn't be reached, and didn't seem in any way interested in her best friend's most joyous occasion.

Because of my daily proximity to the bride, I heard all the gory details, and how understandably upset she was about the situation. Being the overly sympathetic type (people come up to me in airports, supermarkets, hotels, and even the lobby of my own building to tell me their life stories and ask for advice), I ended up being the Dear Abby of the wedding circuit, at least in that circle.

Also because I was right under her nose, the bride asked me to go look at bridal gowns, watch her try to crowbar herself into the impossible samples, try on bridesmaid dresses, look for shoes, headgear, and every other type of wedding accoutrement you could think of. Living where we do, and working near several huge shopping malls, we were surrounded by a variety of wedding shops and accessory stores, and suddenly my life was no longer my own. I now had a part-time volunteer job, with no compensation of any kind, and no time for myself. I could barely squeeze in time for my other friend's plans, even though I was her maid of honor!

As one would expect with such drama, the mother of the bride was also a drama queen. She didn't like the bridesmaid dress we picked out, which was actually quite elegant and which I used several times after cutting it to street length. The color we chose was too dark for her ladyship, and we'd have to start over. Somehow we found a gorgeous alternative, which Mama also didn't like, but after lots of negotiation by the bride, Mom relented.

Then came the shower. The missing-in-action maid of honor had by now totally decamped, so it fell to her ladyship to plan the event. She came up with a lavish brunch affair in a swanky restaurant that had a party room, and then charged us each our share. Unbelievable. No party in someone's house for this stylish lot, no home-made tea sandwiches for her ladyship; people might talk! But we got through it somehow.

By now, the price tag for this event was starting to match the national debt, at least on my tiny salary.

As the day drew near, the bride kept adding items to the list of things we had to buy and wear, and finally she hit on special gloves. When my raised eyebrows reached around the back of my head she blurted out, "My father will pay for them." This became a mantra, as she began to realize that this part-time job was becoming burden-some for those of us without trust funds or beginner stock portfolios.

By this time, my father, who witnessed my endless shopping trips and phone calls, joked that he was going to get me business cards that said Professional Bridesmaid. I probably could have been a fantastic wedding planner by the time I was done with all of my friends' weddings, if I'd have been able to stand it a minute longer!

I was counting the minutes until this excruciating af-fair was over. My parents were invited to the wedding and attended only because I begged to have at least some sane people present. For years afterward, my fa-ther mimicked the giant toothy grin of the bride's father as he stood on the sidelines surveying the guests dancing. It was an affair to remember, and nobody was happier than I was to wave good-bye to the happy couple!

SURVIVAL HINTS

1. If your friends can't afford the time or money, then don't ask them to be in your wedding.
2. If you're the bride, don't expect people to spend a fortune living your dream. If you want extras, pay for them yourself.
3. Be careful who you choose to be your maid of honor, because she has to run the show and it's not fair to expect the other bridesmaids to pick up the slack.
4. Try to limit the amount of time you expect your bridesmaids to spend shopping and helping you. They have lives too, and they're entitled to spend them on their own pursuits.
5. Minimize your friends' exposure to personal dramas. It can sour them on your family and could make them reevaluate your friendship.

The Unconscious Bride

Barbara A. Craig

THE BRIDE WAS diabetic. She also liked to party, often overdoing it and drinking quite a lot. It wasn't a good combination, to say the least. I was one of her bridesmaids, and as the wedding day got closer, she began more and more to drink to excess, perhaps from nerves, stress, or excitement. I was worried about her diabetes, fearing she could lapse into a diabetic coma and no one would realize it. And she seemed to be getting into that state all too frequently.

On the wedding day, by the time the ceremony was over, and after taking pictures in the hot sun, we were all nearly dying of thirst. Next came the cocktail hour. I asked for water, and when it never came, I drank champagne instead—which went right to my head. By now I was worried about the bride, plus drunk and hungry. What a combination! But once I started to eat and was finally getting some fluids, I could stop worrying about turning into a pile of dust in the middle of the dance floor. My mood lifted—at least for the moment.

Soon I was actually having a good time—that is, until the bride's grandmother came to get me. That's when I found out the bride had passed out cold on the ladies' room floor. I helped her obnoxious mother and new husband get her to a couch, but we couldn't wake her up. I was concerned about her diabetes, sinceI knew a diabetic man who passed out from one beer too many—only to wake up blind. He told me he was lucky to have woken up at all.

When I insisted that we call an ambulance for our drunken newlywed, her mother and her new husband told me I was being silly. When I pointed out that she was drunk, diabetic, and not responding, they told me they knew what was best for her and to mind my own business. Her mother hissed that she was only passed out from the excitement over her wedding. At this point, I realized they both were in denial. I told her that her daughter had a serious problem, and she needed to get help. But the new husband was also a drinker, and he wouldn't want her to stop, so it wasn't likely anything would change. When the bride's grandmother agreed with me, they told her to stay out of it, too.

Then, to my amazement, after all this, the bride's mother asked if I would go around and collect the gift cards on behalf of the couple! After I had taken care of this important detail, the mother of the bride and the groom then dragged his unconscious and bedraggled bride outside to take her home. She survived, but how much the bride remembered of her special day I'll never know. She might have enjoyed it more if she'd indulged a little less.

SURVIVAL HINTS

1. If you're in a wedding party and have issues with the behavior of one of the principals, it might be best to bow out early, rather than deal with the dramas that might unfold as the big day draws near.
2. If you're concerned about a friend's drinking and health, it's probably best to talk about it with them when you first notice the problem, rather than waiting until there's a crisis.

6

When Friends and Family Are Making a Scene

Sanity Quiz

It's your big day. You've dreamed about your wedding since you were a young girl. You've pictured the flowers, the gown, the dancing, and the man you love. What you never pictured was an unruly family member creating a scene at your wedding. Up until now, that is. But right now, your crazy cousin Blake is making a spectacle out of himself. He's drunk from spending too much time at the open bar, and is now disrobing on the dance floor like some sort of Chippendales reject.

Do you
A. politely ask him to leave the reception
B. run and hide in the bathroom to escape the embarrassment
C. ask the DJ to play a striptease tune
D. go out and shake your booty with him

No matter how you answered this question, you haven't even begun to know what can happen when guests go haywire. Read and learn.

The Bad Wedding Singer

C. J. Fallon

IT TOOK ME two years to plan my wedding. I was a perfectionist. I made sure every detail was taken care of, then double-checked. Most of all I wanted a smooth run, right down to choosing the band that would play at the reception. We went to hear over twenty before we finally picked the one we knew was right for us. But as with planning any event that involves a large number of people, you can be sure that something somewhere will go awry.

The ceremony itself was lovely. The pictures following the ceremony were borderline. We had chosen a beautiful monastery because of the gorgeous grounds. But it had rained pretty hard the day before and, while taking the pictures, the bridesmaids' lavender spikes had started to sink rapidly. But that was nothing compared to what happened at the reception.

What took the cake was when my aunt Rita insisted the band let her preteenage daughter, Jamie, belt out the tune "Heart of Gold" by Neil Young. If you've ever heard someone scratch their nails across a blackboard, it would have been a serious improvement to Cousin Jamie's singing. It was awful: People were sitting at their tables looking around, wondering where that horrible noise was coming from. The band members were shaking their own heads all the way through. I ran out of the ballroom and into the bathroom to hide. I didn't know what to do. I just wanted the horror to stop.

Jamie clearly couldn't hold a tune. Knowing full well that I had to go back in there and face the music (so to speak), I quickly pulled myself together and, with my head high, reentered the ballroom. Jamie was still wailing away, with my aunt Rita watching, proud as a large peacock. She had pulled up a chair right in front of the stage. There she sat, smiling away.

My first thoughts were, You must be deaf, lady. That kid can't sing! My second thought was, Well, you gotta live with her. And lastly I thought, How rude is it to interrupt someone else's wedding without permission, simply to give her chubby little no-talent daughter a shot in the spotlight. But rather than let it ruin my special day and my future memories thereof, I decided to just brush the whole thing off.

Just as an update, I am preparing to marry off my first son this fall. I haven't seen Aunt Rita in over ten years, so I don't think I will be inviting her. And as for Jamie, as far as I know, she never became a rock star. But if you see a large, red-haired woman and a short, plump brunette heading for the microphone at your wedding, look out. Last I heard they were trying to go on tour!

SURVIVAL HINTS

1. Don't be afraid to tell the band—no guest performers unless they clear it with you first!
2. No matter what goes wrong at your wedding, don't let anyone or anything get to you. It's your day—enjoy it.

Is That Aunt Ruby, or Just Part of Her in Those Photos?

Sally Manning

YOU WOULDN'T THINK you would have to enforce a dress code for your wedding, but now I surely wish I had. Most people who attend weddings dress in their best for the gala event. And you can usually count on someone who will dress in something that will stand out from the rest. For me it was Aunt Ruby. Now, on any other occasion, it wouldn't have offended me, but this was above and beyond even the wildest of imaginations. And I have the wedding pictures to prove it.

Aunt Ruby was a large woman. She weighed about 250 pounds, was damn near six feet tall, had carrot-red hair, and a set of the largest breasts I had ever seen, even by Dolly Parton standards. Get the picture? You couldn't have missed her if you tried.

Well, not only was Aunt Ruby a big woman but she always seemed to try twice as hard to attract lots of attention to herself. She was loud, with a deep, masculine voice, argumentative, and dressed like a hooker. Yes, I said a hooker. "Revealing" was her motto—that, and making sure to leave another button undone to expose just a little extra of her watermelons that were already halfway out of her blouse. Aunt Ruby was married and she wasn't on a manhunt, so I really never understood why she did this. Whatever the reason, she always seemed to make a spectacle of herself.

There is a time and place for everything and my wedding certainly wasn't the venue for her leopard jumpsuit with the V-neck that exposed a line to her navel and a little bit of everything else along the way. Not to mention that it was semi-see-through. Aunt Ruby was also the queen of bra burners. Her boobs flapped in the wind like a kite on a cold winter's day.

The wedding photographer I hired by referral was a little dweeby-looking man who apparently had a fascination with breasts. I went picture by picture through my wedding album: I probably have equal numbers of Aunt Ruby's gems as of me and my husband. The best one of all includes my husband and me at the altar and Aunt Ruby's left one hanging over the church pew!

I found out too late that the person I had trusted to give me the referral to the wedding photographer was actually getting a kickback. I learned that it's best not to take anyone's word for anything when it comes to wedding photographers.

SURVIVAL HINTS

1. If you have a guest coming to your wedding who has questionable or overly risqué taste, try to find out what they plan on wearing to avoid embarrassment. Obviously this can be a touchy subject, so handle with care!

2. Do your research before hiring someone to capture your special moments. This should include seeing samples of their work from several other weddings. It also wouldn't hurt to ask for references from past customers. After all, unless you plan on getting married more than once, you only have one shot at getting the wedding album you hope for.

Do I Know You?

Lori Banlovitch

PLANNING A WEDDING isn't easy, and one of the most difficult tasks is selecting the final guest list. My fiancé and I didn't want a huge wedding, and we wanted to stick to our chosen number of 125 guests.

My parents were paying for the wedding and I felt strongly about *not* emptying their pockets for my benefit. My mother had insisted she was taking care of everything and that it was okay to splurge. But I still wasn't comfortable with going crazy and overspending. After all, we wanted an intimate wedding, not the Macy's Thanksgiving Day Parade. Well, at least I didn't.

I come from a large family and so does my husband. So paring down the guest list from everyone we knew to 125 was quite the task. We started by eliminating family members we didn't see on a regular basis, those who lived far away, those we hadn't heard from in years, or with whom we'd lost touch. That was the easy part. Well, it was easy for me, but not so easy for my husband-to-be. He felt that we should invite some of his distant cousins whom he hadn't seen in years. I explained to him that it just wasn't possible.

The cost of the wedding was becoming excessive, right up to the limit of our budget. It was quite a chunk of change, and I was adamant about staying within the bounds I'd set. I didn't want my parents having to spend anything more than necessary. So we agreed this was it, and no matter how uncomfortable the selection process became, we had to stick to our limit.

Also included in that 125-person head count was our wedding party and our closest friends. The seating chart was a seat-by-seat maze. Getting through it without hurting anyone's feelings and coming up with the people nearest and dearest to us was tough. But we got there. Many discussions and checklists later, we were finished at last.

The invitations went out and time flew by. Finally it was our wedding day. The wedding went off as planned. That is, right up until the reception. We had a full house. All 125 invited guests had attended. The reception was held in the ballroom of one of the best restaurants around. It was a grand-looking room with several crystal chandeliers that hung from the high ceiling, creating the softest glimmer of light and the proper ambiance for this special event. It could not have been more beautiful.

As the party went on, guests continued to come to the head table to offer their congratulations. We were enjoying a glass of champagne when a couple approached with a card and their good wishes. We accepted and they then went off to dance. I looked at my husband, perplexed. I had no idea who these two people were. At first I thought they may just have been some relatives of his who I had never met, but the way he was acting told me different.

"Who were they?" I asked.

"Ah, that's just Becky and Bob," he said.

I asked, "Who are Becky and Bob?"

"They hang out at the Hotel once in a while," he replied. The Hotel is a local bar, the same establishment where my husband and I first met.

"Who the hell invited them?" I questioned.

"I don't know," he said, "I didn't."

I was getting madder by the minute. I'd never seen these two people before in my life. What were they doing at my wedding? We'd had to leave some of our own friends and family off the guest list so we could keep to our agreed number, and now I had two complete strangers at my wedding! I was furious. I told him to go find out who'd invited them or I would have them removed. I couldn't believe it. This may have been the first time my husband saw just how mad I could get.

In the meantime, while my husband was cruising the ballroom floor looking for answers, ole Becky and Bob decided it was time to really get out there on the dance floor and cut some rug. I couldn't believe what I was seeing. They were taking up the whole dance floor in some kind of swing routine; they were all over each other. The rest of the crowd was being shoved off to the side. Now I was really mad. In fact, mad may have been an understatement.

Just then, my new husband slunk back up to the head table to tell me what he had found out. His first words were, "Now don't get mad."

"Get mad!" I said. "I *am* mad!"

"Ben invited them." Ben being his best man.

"Ben?" I asked. "Why would Ben think it's okay for him to invite someone to my wedding?" I belted back.

"He was drunk last night at the Hotel and they were sitting with him and he mentioned it. They wanted to come so he said they could."

"What?" I yelled. By this time the color of my skin, which is normally quite fair, had changed to blood-pressure-on-the-rise red.

Now, I wasn't all that fond of Ben to begin with back then. He seemed to always go out of his way to cause trouble between my husband and me. But this was the last straw. I was furious. I told him to go tell both Becky and Bob to pack it up and get the hell out, and while he was at it he could tell Ben to follow them, otherwise I would. And I promised him it wouldn't be pretty. He did everything he could to change my mind, including making Ben apologize. But at this point I had had enough. I didn't want to hear it.

The crowd had obviously noticed my change in color and had begun to wonder what was going on. Just then Manny, one of my husband's ushers and a close friend, came to talk to me. Manny is a big guy, very calm, kind of a gentle-giant type.

He said, "Don't let it bother you. It's your day, not theirs."

After a good rant about why I was so mad and him listening intently, I felt better and came to the conclusion that Manny was right. This was my day and it wasn't going to be ruined by them or anyone else. So they all stayed at the party and Ben now owes me one—for life.

SURVIVAL HINT

1. If you think you might attract gate-crashers at your wedding, have the hotel, restaurant, or caterer check names off the guest list.
2. If someone unexpected shows up, designate someone diplomatic to handle it so you don't have to deal with anything unpleasant on your special day.

Out of Sync

Ginny Chandoha

MY HUSBAND HAS a penchant for tardiness. Invariably he is late for work, and on the weekends, he never really gets going until the afternoon. Since I am one of those people who wake up instantly, I can have a whole day's worth of work done by the time he's just getting started.

If we were to travel to a family gathering for holidays or special occasions, even though he'd be aware of the deadline, he'd wait until we were ready to walk out the door to do the maintenance on the car. It never seemed to fail that we would be leaving the house around the time I'd promised we'd be arriving at our destination.

Since he always seemed out of sync with the rest of the world, I came to refer to his scheduling as "Chandoha time." To try to synchronize his time with deadlines, I took to telling him we were due at a certain place at least an hour or two ahead of the actual time. On occasion, I even pushed a due date up by a day, in the hope that the automobile maintenance would be accomplished ahead of schedule.

This worked well for quite some time, until we were invited to attend a friend's spring wedding in another state. John made sure the alarm was set several hours early to afford him plenty of time to get ready, and the car was checked out a week in advance. We even left in plenty of time to drive to the chapel without having to rush. I was quite proud of myself for having accomplished this coup of timeliness.

In fact, we arrived a half hour early, and congratulated ourselves profusely for having pulled off this miracle. We spent the extra time using the local bathroom facilities and adjusting our hair and clothing, being slightly disheveled from the long drive.

We took our time walking to the chapel. I wondered aloud where everyone was, as there were plenty of cars parked all around, but no one in sight, and none of the visible activity that usually accompanies a wedding about to take place. I double-checked the directions to make sure we were in the right place, at the right time. We were.

As we approached the chapel, to our shock, the chapel door opened, and out came the wedding party, along with all the guests who were lining up to greet the new husband and wife.

We had forgotten that the wedding took place on the very spring weekend the clocks were pushed ahead an hour. We were still on "Chandoha time," and even though we were early, we were still late!

SURVIVAL HINTS

1. If your wedding takes place on the day when the time changes, be sure to remind your guests in the invitation.
2. If some of your guests show up late because of a mix-up, don't let it throw you or ruin your day. Besides, it's probably a good story, so encourage them to tell you the truth!

Surviving as Mother of the Bride

Mia Hill

THE DAY HAD finally arrived. It had been well over a year in the planning, with lots of fun and pain, aggravation and excitement, but that is to be expected when your only daughter gets married, and especially when the parents of both the bride and the groom are divorced.

Many aspects of planning the wedding were difficult, but one in particular was exasperating—the reception seating plan. There must have been thirty or forty faxes sent back and forth between the groom's father, Hank, and me. You see, he was very concerned that the tables of people he had invited to the wedding not be anywhere near the tables of people that his first wife, Margaret, had invited.

Well, there is only one room and it is only so big. We finally agreed that Hank's tables would be concentrated in the center of the room. Margaret's tables would be on the right side of the room facing the band. My tables would be on the left side. When I looked at the finalized plan, I laughed. There was no way that Hank's guests could leave the room, for whatever reason, including using the restrooms, without traveling through Margaret's enemy territory. I decided not to share that observation with Hank.

This was not to be so much a wedding as it was to be the celebration of two beautiful people, very much in love. The role of the mother of the bride (Isn't it strange that there is no single word for that significant designation?) is to do everything possible to make that celebration happen smoothly and otherwise stay out of the way. Well, I tried. I seriously tried, but as is typical with complex celebrations, things don't always go as we plan, even for the most organized of us. This wedding turned out to be a very "interesting" experience—for all kinds of reasons.

At last the all-important wedding weekend began. That's right—one night is no longer enough for such a momentous occasion. Rather, an entire weekend of merriment at a country inn had been planned, and indeed it was just that, but with a few twists and turns.

The main event was, of course, to be held on Saturday night, when the marriage ceremony and the celebratory reception were to take place. On Saturday afternoon, starting at about 3:30 P.M., things were buzzing at the inn. As always before a wedding this was a crucial, hectic, and stressful time. Everyone has to shower and be coiffed, made up, and adorned, even the mother of the bride. So, clearing my head of the details of the events by leaving them to the professionals, I headed for my room for an hour of peaceful, solitary, and studied preparation. I knew that I would have that hour because the bride and her maid of honor would be preparing themselves in the bridal suite. They both were expected at my door in just enough time for the bride to don her gown and the veil, which were currently deposited in my room, since it was the closest to where the ceremony was to take place.

At last I enjoyed some moments of blessed silence, peace, and a rare chance to be alone. I stood for a moment, delighted not to have to speak to or smile at anyone for just a little while. I toyed with the thought of a ten-minute nap, but rejected that plan in favor of a long hot shower. And then it began. First I heard a knock at the door. My reaction was one of horror! Next, a key turned in the lock, the door opened, and in waltzed the bride, her maid of honor, the hairdresser hired for the big day, and a few of the bride's close friends. Plans had obviously changed! Hair and makeup were now to be done in my little room cum salon, because the bridal suite had been commandeered by those dressing the groom.

As the bride's dressing entourage set up their paint, powders, pencils, brushes, and whatnot, I decided to take a very fast shower. Here I was in the shower, with shampoo in my eyes, when all of a sudden an arm, holding a glass, reached in through the shower curtain. Attached to the arm was Amy, the wedding photographer who also happened to be a close friend of the groom's father's new wife, Susan. Thanks Amy, this really is exactly what I need right now, vodka on the rocks mid-shower!

I got out of the shower fast—noting that my legs were bleeding from my having done my usual miserable job of shaving them—when there was a knock on the bath-room door. I wrapped myself in a towel and opened the door to find Margaret, the groom's mother, already dressed, made up, and gorgeous. "I just stopped by to say much happiness," as she planted a kiss on my wet face and closed the door.

I hurriedly dried myself, fixed my hair, applied my makeup, put on a bathrobe, and went into the room, ignoring my bloody legs. Next came another knock at the door. "I came to change my clothes," said Belinda, the groom's aunt, as she pushed her way in. "I didn't want to drive all the way here sitting in my dress." She turned to me and said, "So *this* is the great Mrs. Hill!" I looked at her and inside my head I began to scream, Don't you remember my name? (I must also confess that the use of the title "Mrs." offends me. I have not been Mrs. anybody for a long time, first because I am divorced, and second because I have a doctorate.) I guess I was strained by that point because I responded to her greeting with, "You can call me Mia or you can call me Dr. Hill, but you cannot address me as Mrs. because that is not my name." Belinda responded with, "La-di-da. Aren't you fancy?" Having by now changed her clothes, she exited the chaos of my room.

By this point, all that remained was for me to put on my dress. I looked down at my stockings to discover that blood was still running from the shaving cuts on my legs and simply refused to stop. Just then came the next knock at the door. My sister and her daughter had stopped in to say hello. Well, my sister instantly took charge. Three cold towels and several Band-Aids later, we were finally just about ready to head for the ceremony. What else could possibly happen?

The ceremony was beautiful. I was both happy and tearful as my daughter and her groom recited their pledges to each other. At last they were husband and wife. The band began to play as the bride and groom made their way up the aisle, with everyone on their feet offering congratulations. Then, out of the corner of my eye, I spied Susan, the groom's stepmother, walk up to the bandstand with a microphone. To my surprise, she began singing an old Al Jolson song, "Another bride, another groom, another sunny honeymoon, another season, another reason for making whoopee." All four verses ending with, "You better keep her, I think it's cheaper than making whoopee." I glanced at my friend Irma, who was rolling her eyes. I was sufficiently dumbstruck. Some people were standing with their mouths open while others cheered loudly. What a strange sentiment for starting a marriage!

But soon the wedding feast was going well and most of Hank's people somehow negotiated the path to the restroom, through enemy territory, without visible harm. The music was hot and spicy—this was no typical wedding band—as the bride and groom had selected a rock band. Everyone was dancing, drinking, and just generally having fun.

Having performed all my appointed duties, I also wanted to have some fun, which I felt was my due. So I headed out to the dance floor, clasped hands with the bride, and we began to dance together. I turned to the right and then around to face the bride—but I never made it back around. The best man's leg tripped me and down I went. It was only a split second before I was picked up and put back on my feet. I smiled but something was definitely wrong. I was in *pain!* My right arm was useless. "Wow," I thought, "am I glad I took off my jacket before I got up to dance." If there is any doubt about how this episode unfolded, it remains captured for posterity and is clearly visible on the wedding video! The best man has not lived it down to this day, although I still speak to him.

I was walked back to my table where my friends gathered. Patti, one of my oldest friends, had recently taken a first-aid course. She took one look at me and immediately ran to find some magazines. She returned and placed one magazine on each side of my right arm, and then tied them in place with napkins. The evening was still young and I had no intention of going anywhere, so I remained at the reception and continued to drink vodka, which seemed to help quite a bit. My only concession was that I didn't return to the dangers of the dance floor.

Finally, when everyone had gone home, my sister and brother-in-law drove me to the emergency room at a nearby hospital. I was amazed that the orthopedic surgeon on call arrived at the hospital so quickly and in good spirits, because by now it was three in the morning. A few X-rays and a plaster cast later, I was ready to return to the country inn. Only now my right arm was permanently bent at the elbow, with a cast extending from the top of my fingernails to my armpit. At least my manicure still looked good!

Back at the inn, I followed the noise to the bridal suite. There was an after-wedding party in progress for close friends of the couple. When I walked in, my daughter, taking one look at me, said, "Only my mother!" But she came to my room the next morning to help me to dress for the brunch being given for those who had stayed overnight at the inn.

At last, after all the festivities had come to a close, I was on my way back home, where I could take the time to dress myself and put on makeup and mascara in order to go back to work the next day. All in all, it was a memorable wedding weekend, and I somehow survived being mother of the bride—just by the skin of my teeth!

SURVIVAL HINTS

1. Stay calm no matter what happens.
2. Smile a lot, no matter how you are feeling.
3. Remember that this is your child and this is a very special day that will never happen again.
4. Remember that you do not have to see the in-laws often after the wedding.
5. Try to think only pleasant thoughts about this very special event.
6. Look forward to seeing all the people you really love at the celebration.
7. Remember that it will all be just a memory very soon, no matter how crazy you're being driven.
8. Did I say to remain calm?

My Daughter's Wedding

Ashna Sesky

MY BEAUTIFUL, SMART daughter's first—and broken—engagement was a bad experience, and luckily
things ended in time. Afterward she finally found Mr.
Right, but let's talk first about that engagement to Mr.
Wrong.

My daughter met her beloved on the east end of
Montauk. He was a cook in a renowned restaurant there,
and she was also working at a restaurant. He was handsome and charming to be sure, gracious when he met us,
and they seemed very much in love.

When the summer season ended, I hosted an engagement party for them. He had lost his mom when he was
very young, and he and his brother had been raised by
their dad.

He did not have a very large extended family, and because of his occupation, he had little time to interact with our family, nor did he have much time to share the holidays. I worried about this but my daughter, being in the same profession at the time, was unconcerned. The party was a family dinner, quiet and understated. The family brought gifts and all seemed to go well.

Several days later my daughter called me and told me the wedding was off. They had differences of opinion about family, responsibilities, commitment, etc. She came to my office, very upset, crying, disappointed, but very sure of her decision. And I too agreed that this would have been a difficult union because the restaurateur's life isn't an easy one, and it's hard to include a family in the future.

We had just about calmed down, agreed that she'd made the right decision, when she went into our front office and realized that someone had stolen her purse—which held her wallet, ID, money, credit cards, and everything else in her bag.

This was the topper. She flipped and so did I. I told her I would take her into town to the bank to get money, to a luggage store that sold wallets and handbags, and to the police to report the theft. Reluctantly she went along. Her eyes were red from crying and she felt miserable.

On our way out of the bank we ran into my jeweler. I introduced my daughter, and he took one look at her, with her bloodshot eyes, and asked, "What happened to you?" Teary-eyed, she said that her engagement was broken and someone had just stolen her handbag. He said the following: "Don't cry kid, you're not ugly, you're not pregnant, you'll find a new guy, and your mom will buy you a new wallet and get you some money."

Both of us got hysterical with laughter. How funny he was, how right he was, and it seemed that everything from then on would be okay.

Several years later she met her *b'sheret*. He was the brother of her best girlfriend. They had known each other for years and had never connected, but as guests at another friend's wedding, they found each other.

He, her *b'sheret*, didn't yet have his career in place, but nonetheless they worked together to establish a solid relationship and soon planned to marry. At this time my husband was having severe back pain and was contemplating surgery. I also had my business to run, and very little extra time, and now my daughter was off making plans for a wedding. We made a deal: She could plan her wedding and I would have some say in the gown and the plans.

My husband had the surgery, followed by a long recuperation, and my daughter's future mother-in-law was instrumental in helping my daughter with the invitations and flowers through her family connections.

The gown, according to our agreement, was to be selected at my approval, and we went to a bridal shop in town. She tried on a gown I loved. She then told me she wanted to show it to her future mother-in-law. I went ballistic. I said, out loud, much to my daughter's dismay: "I'm paying for this and your future mother-in-law has nothing to say in this matter."

My daughter, the diplomat, understanding the stress I was under, ordered the gown and said no more about it. Needless to say, she looked gorgeous. She was slim, tan, pretty, and full of personality. And the dress was perfect for her.

So they were married, and now, eleven years later, they have a home, great jobs, and three beautiful, smart, charming children—my grandchildren, all of whom I adore. We never really know what the future holds. The best thing to do is just be there for your kids and follow the bouncing ball. With luck and love, everything will turn out right.

7

When Disaster Strikes, or Your Vendors Let You Down

Is That Seafood Newburg or Bait on My Buffet?
Danielle Fracas

A Place for Everyone
Marcy Vandertel

When Your Hotel Won't Cooperate, or When East Meets Midwest
Ken Hastie

Capturing the Memories
Cindy Matchett

Sanity Quiz

You've chosen the prettiest white roses for your wedding. It's the morning of the big event and your florist delivers the beauties just in time. Opening the boxes you cannot believe the horror before your eyes! The flowers are completely wilted and ruined. Turns out the florist's freezer went on the blink and froze everything solid.

Do you
A. demand a refund and use a dining room centerpiece as your bouquet
B. cry yourself a river
C. run out in the yard and clip a few flowers off the bushes by the church
D. carry something else, like a bottle of tissues because you can't stop crying over the flowers
E. call the whole thing off

If you answered yes to any of these questions, you'll be able to appreciate what our contributors learned when things didn't go according to plan.

The Bad Wedding Photographer

Mary Corbett

IN MY THIRTY-SEVEN years on this Earth, I have only one regret.

I don't regret that I started smoking for absolutely no reason and still—after twenty years—can't seem to completely kick the habit of being a social smoker. Why would I? I've got it under control. Besides, with a drink in one hand and a cigarette in another, I make for a fun party guest.

I don't regret dating a parade of fools during my twenties who (a) broke my heart, (b) crippled my self-esteem, (c) turned me into a wine-guzzling, drunk-dialing Bridget Jones, or (d) all of the above. Why would I? Eventually, all of those lessons learned led me to my great husband.

I don't regret not applying myself during my entire seventeen years of schooling. What do a few snide comments on my third-grade report card about "Mary not applying herself" mean now?

The only regret I have in my life is that I hired the wrong wedding photographer.

In May of 1999, I met my husband, Jon, at a neighborhood meeting. It was a whirlwind romance and we were engaged in ten days. I wasn't pregnant and he wasn't a stalker or a serial killer. We just immediately fell in love and wanted to get married. Imagine that!

We decided that we would have a nine-month engagement so that our families and friends could recover from the shock and hopefully tire of whispering "It will never last" by the time our wedding ceremony rolled around.

The wedding would be simple and elegant. It was my second wedding (Jon's first) and since I wasn't a soap opera character or a Hollywood star, I didn't think it appropriate for a second-time bride to throw herself a Bridezilla affair twice. We'll leave that to Joan Lunden. However, I didn't want to spoil things for Jon and his family. After all, he wasn't a sinner in the eyes of the Catholic Church like me. Why should he be punished?

Jon and I agreed that a scaled-down affair would be best. Regardless of my Scarlet Letter A, we were both over thirty and didn't want a stiff, traditional, or big wedding. However, we wanted the day to be elegant in every way. And "elegant" costs money! Less *is* more.

We made our guest list and estimated that ninety close friends and family members would attend. We booked the small chapel at our downtown church for a Friday night in February. We worked closely with our wonderful priest, Father Forlitti—who somehow managed to get my annulment through in three months flat—to plan the perfect ceremony.

We didn't do a full-blown bridal registry; it just wouldn't have been appropriate. Besides, I had enough Pyrex. But Jon, a military guy, picked out our gorgeous Lincoln Pickard china. He fell in love with it because it was made in America, was used in the White House, and even had a flag on the back. The fact that $225 was way over the amount that our Minnesota guests would spend didn't faze us one bit. To hell with 'em.

We selected elegant engraved Crane invitations that only paper snobs like us could appreciate. A top florist carefully copied a minimal nosegay of miniature calla lilies that I spotted on the cover of Martha Stewart's wedding magazine. Our square chocolate and raspberry cake (which Jon and his mom picked out) was iced in white butter cream.

And, of course, there was the dress. It wasn't fluffy. It wasn't fancy. But it was custom designed especially for me. The fabric was amazing and fit like a glove. Topped with a brocade winter coat that was trimmed in fake white fur, I would be the perfect winter bride. My Swarovski crystal hair jewelry completed the look.

Everything was set. It would be the perfect day.

And it was. It was perfect. Too bad I don't have one decent photograph to prove it.

Even five years later, when I allow myself to think about it, the regret just weighs me down. I had always dreamed of having the perfect husband and the perfect leather-bound book of photographs to show to our perfect children. If there were ever a fire, I would take the album out from under my pillow, clutch it to my breast, and be ready to give my life for it (after the kids were safe, that is). Instead, I have a stack of 3 x 5 photos piled in a shoe box sitting at the bottom of Jon's closet. Every time I see that damn box my heart starts and I want to kick a hole in the wall. Or, at least smoke a cigarette. It just makes me so sad.

The most frustrating part of this misfortune is that I did everything in my power to make sure that we would have *great* wedding photos. At the time, couples were trading in traditional wedding photographers for a more stylistic, journalistic approach. My friend Linda had discovered a very talented amateur photographer to do her wedding photos. The woman delivered in spades. When I saw the beautiful black-and-white photographs that soulfully captured every detail of Linda's big day, I knew that I wanted to take the same approach. Since our wedding was on a Friday evening, and we didn't have a wedding party, head table, or any of the traditional trappings, I couldn't see hiring a traditional photographer. I didn't want to spend the time posing for a bunch of pictures and the thought of my face superimposed in a champagne glass just didn't seem to fit what Jon and I were going for.

Of course, when we married, three years after Linda, her photographer was no longer an amateur. She was a sought-after wedding photographer who commanded more than fifteen hundred dollars a day. I thought about hiring her but just wasn't sure about spending that much money. Besides, I had connections. I was the director of marketing at a large architecture firm and hired top professional photographers everyday. I was also a high-profile volunteer at a very chichi Twin Cities photography gallery. I decided to hire the gallery director to do our wedding photos. I paid Vince eight hundred dollars. I figured that two hundred dollars an hour wasn't anything to sneeze at.

As I waited in the vestibule before walking down the aisle, I wondered where Vince was. It would have been nice for him to get some pictures of me primping with my sisters in the bathroom. But I reasoned that he was probably with Jon and that it was far better that he be waiting for me at the end of the aisle.

When I heard the procession music swell, I couldn't believe what I was hearing (Jon selected the music). I walked down the aisle to an orchestrated version of the theme from the movie *Babe*—yes, the movie about the pig! I clutched the hands of my three-year-old flower girls and started my walk down the aisle. Suddenly, I heard somebody behind me say, "Mary!" I turned around and was blinded by a flashbulb. There was Vince, happy as can be, even though he was obviously late. I smiled at him quickly and turned around to continue walking. I remember thinking to myself "If he is in back of me, then he isn't in front of me." Good thing my small train was pretty.

The next time I saw Vince was after walking through the arch of sabers (the million dollar picture), but he only snapped one quick shot. At the woman's club reception, he seemed to be in on all the action. But he also seemed to be enjoying the open bar. I remember posing for a few pictures with our family members and with Jon at the end of the evening (when my lipstick was but a memory and my dress had a red wine stain on it), but everything else was a blur. My concern was replaced by confidence. After all, I had seen him snapping pictures all night long. And he was not only a professional, but an artist.

People raved about our wedding. The ceremony was beautiful. The food was divine. The dress was perfect. The cake was as light as air. And, of course, the groom was handsome in his uniform. I couldn't wait to see the pictures.

Soon, Vince called me with good news. The pictures were back and they were great! On our way to the airport for our honeymoon, Jon and I stopped to pick them up. I could hardly wait to see them.

It didn't take me more than thirty seconds to realize that Vince had blown it. He had gone from table to table taking pictures of our guests—and other things. There was an art shot of the chef holding a big knife at the carving station and my flower girl's face reflected in a silver chafing dish. It seemed Vince had taken arts shots of every single person at our wedding—except the bride and groom.

I was devastated. People urged us to re-create the day and get a portrait done in our wedding clothes. But that just seemed so fake because, to me, it was about the day. *That* day. Fake pictures wouldn't have made me feel better.

The only thing that gives me solace is to remember that there was a time when weddings weren't about photographers, videographers, and the like. Weddings were just something that you did so you could be married and start a life together. A woman had one portrait in her wedding dress and one portrait with her new husband and that was about it. And somehow, those few precious images outlive any one day. The convenience of paging through a perfect wedding album and pointing out all the elegant details is replaced by asking the bride about her wedding. And since that bride, like me, doesn't have pictures, she recounts how she felt on that day.

I don't need pictures to remember how I felt on that day. I felt that I was the luckiest woman in the world because I was going to be Jon's wife.

So I hired the wrong wedding photographer. But I married the right man. And that I will never regret.

SURVIVAL HINTS

1. Let the groom make some of the major decisions
   . . . your wedding will be much more unique.
2. Try not to smoke in your wedding dress. It is very
   unbecoming and you don't want it captured on
   film!
3. If pictures are important to you, cut back on
   something else and spend the money on a reliable
   wedding photographer.
4. Planning a wedding is stressful, but nothing
   compared to maintaining a healthy, happy
   marriage. Put it in perspective.
5. Your wedding is *not* the best day of your life—the
   best day of your life is when you know that you
   have married the right person.

The Incapacitated Father-in-Law

Pam Brodowsky

YES, YOU READ it right. *Incapacitated.* It didn't happen before we announced the wedding, of course. Instead, the incapacitating event waited until about two weeks before the wedding, and one week before my father-in-law had his final fitting for his tuxedo.

You see, I come from and married into a family of do-it-yourselfers. Everything from building it, to tearing it down, cutting down trees, splitting your own firewood, plowing your own driveway, you name it, they do it. Hey, why not, if you can save a buck or two?

Let me tell you why not. About two weeks before our wedding there was a hefty snowstorm. It was heavy, but really what can you expect for the month of March? What sane person would pick the month of March to get married in? Really, I can't even remember why we chose that month. Most likely it was because my husband didn't want our wedding interfering with the beginning of trout season. Yes, ladies, I married one of those.

So to make a long story short, my father-in-law decided to plow the driveway on 'Ole Faithful, a tractor equipped with four-wheel drive that had been given to him by *his* father, another die-hard do-it-yourselfer.

Now, he is a pro at this and has been doing it for years. After all, when your driveway is over a quarter of a mile long and all uphill, you'd better know how to plow the damn thing yourself. Otherwise, forget about getting up the driveway on the mountain in Pennsylvania for at least six months of the year. Going down the hill is fine, but getting up the hill in ice or snow is something few would attempt. I know. I've often been stuck on that hill.

So on the night in question (remember it's only a week until the final tux fitting), my future father-in-law, after returning home from work and eating his supper, decided that he had better go out and plow. He told Shirley, my future mother-in-law, that he was headed out and would be back in awhile. The next time Shirley saw him, he was on his elbows, flat on his belly, crawling into the house. This was the method he'd used to get himself all the way up the quarter-mile drive.

And this wasn't his first injury. The family is accident prone. All he had done was to jump off of the tractor. But it was the way he had landed on the slippery ground that did the damage that fateful day. It took out his knee along with several ligaments.

Shirley, a petite woman, wasn't able to get him into the car for the trip to the hospital. Stubborn as he is, he refused an ambulance ride. So in order to get him into the car, she called a nearby brother—who luckily had a four-wheel-drive vehicle that could get up the driveway to the house—and had him help her carry her husband to the car.

After hours at the emergency room, my father-in-law left in a cast that went from his thigh to his ankle—a full leg of plaster. And one that just might not fit into a tuxedo pant leg!

I will never forget the phone call I received about two days later. Neither one of them wanted to tell us about the accident. It's just not something you want to say to your kids right before their wedding: "Oh, I'm sorry I busted up my leg, can't walk, and am buried thigh-high in plaster."

My father-in-law made the call himself. It's my guess that Shirley told him he had to. She was not covering for him with the time so short. The call went something like this:

"Hello, this is your favorite father-in-law."

"Well, hello father-in-law," I would say, "This is your favorite daughter-in-law." (Since the two of us are each other's only father- and daughter-in-law, it's pretty much accepted that we are each other's favorite.)

"I have something to tell you," he says.

"What's that?" I say.

"I may have trouble fitting in the tux on Tuesday," he says.

"And why would that be?"

Then he proceeded to tell me the whole story. I felt like a bomb was being dropped on me. What were we going to do at this late date to correct this uncorrectable situation?

I responded in the only way I could: "There has got to be a way to get you and your leg into that tux. And as far as the parent/in-law dance goes, you can dance with a bum leg. I will help to hold you up."

He somehow made it into the tux. I really don't know how they pulled it off. But I am sure glad we had a creative tailor who had a good sense of humor. We also danced that dance without the crutches.

This year his other son is getting married. We have the local ambulance on standby.

SURVIVAL HINTS

1. In planning a wedding it's not just you and your fiancé that you have to worry about, but also everyone who is involved. Accidents and unplanned events happen, and often there are solutions to almost every problem if you look carefully.

2. Be flexible with your plans. Sometimes you end up with a slightly different outcome because of guests' or bridal party situations, but the most important thing is not to let any of it get to you.

The Centerpiece Crisis

Vicky Wells

WHEN MY DAUGHTER, Stephanie, and I started planning her wedding, we hired a florist to prepare bouquets for her and her bridesmaids, and boutonnières for the groomsmen and others in the wedding party. But to "save" money, Stephanie decided to make her own floral centerpieces for the tables at her dinner reception. I know that on the surface this doesn't sound too unusual, or too difficult. But it was.

The bride had envisioned centerpieces using dramatic gladiolus in tall vases. Stephanie loves fish, and so she had another inspiration: Why not add some little fish to the vases, to swim among the gladiolus stems and colorful marbles? Wouldn't that be a stunning centerpiece? Little fish swimming on each table at her reception, now *that* would be a centerpiece to entertain the guests *and* look beautiful.

Conveniently, her future sister-in-law worked in a pet store and could supply us with lots of little fish. The bride planned to acclimate the fish to the centerpieces ahead of time, and scoop out any that did not survive by the day of the wedding. I became alarmed and asked if the gladiolus in the water might not kill the fish? Would we get to the reception and find that some or all of the fish were belly-up? Not a very appetizing prospect at the dinner table!

Months before the wedding, the bride and I had pre-viewed the reception hall with the caterer. The caterer and I thought that low-profile floral arrangements would allow for ease of conversation among the dinner guests seated at the round tables. I imagined simple arrange-ments in low vases with short-stemmed or cut flowers.

But Stephanie, never one to shy away from an artistic challenge, had something else in mind. She felt that even with this new idea of low vases, she could still use gladiolus, although these elegant and striking flowers have stems that stand three feet tall when cut! The bride envisioned an Asian-inspired arrangement with the glad-iolus dramatically crisscrossing within a five-inch tall terrarium bowl filled with colorful marbles. If the bride wants thirty-six-inch flowers arranged in a five-inch vase, who can change her mind? But I was glad to see the fish go when Stephanie agreed to this!

We went on a shopping trip to purchase the supplies for the "simplified" plan: twenty terrarium bowls, twenty floral foam squares, glue, wire, and bags and bags of decorative blue marbles to fill the terrariums. Dozens of gladiolus were placed on order. While shopping, I noticed that we could buy tall glass vases that would easily accommodate the beautiful but top-heavy flowers. I'd forgotten that this was her original idea. I suggested that this would be an easy and foolproof way to display the flowers, but the bride just looked at me like I was crazy.

A few weeks before the wedding, Stephanie bought a test bouquet of gladiolus to try out her floral arrangement idea. As I expected, the glue didn't work, the foam didn't work, and the lengthy gladiolus refused to stay put in the five-inch terrariums. Every attempt to force the flowers to do her bidding ended up in disaster. She shed tears of frustration when nothing seemed to work, but she remained determined. Stephanie tried four different types of glue, different floral foam, and different techniques to get the gladiolus to cooperate. Even worse, the flowers did not last very long: as a matter of fact, they collapsed once water was added to the shallow bowls. I tried to convince her that she had done all she could to make it work, and with the wedding day rapidly approaching, we should switch to the tall glass vases.

Two days before the wedding, Stephanie valiantly made one last concerted attempt to create the centerpiece of her dreams, but to no avail. Finally, on the day before the wedding, the bride decided her unique gladiolus arrangement would not work after all. I breathed a sigh of relief and we ran out to find the twenty tall vases that I had seen a few weeks before. On the morning of the wedding, we brought the vases and gladiolus to the reception hall. We easily arranged the gladiolus in these new vases, to stunning effect. The centerpieces were dramatic, without the aid of glue, foam, and blue marbles—or fish.

And now over a year has passed since the wedding, and Stephanie and I both agree that we learned a lot—and would have done some things differently—if we just knew then what we know now. When I mention the Asian-inspired gladiolus centerpieces, she assures me that it was all my idea, and that she wishes she had just used the tall vases she'd wanted in the first place! Even now she insists that she could have made her gravity-defying centerpiece work.

I stayed sane because I realized the bride is always right!

SURVIVAL HINTS

1. Remember that the bride *is* always right, and if she isn't, you need to be very careful how you dissuade her from a bad idea. You may end up hearing about it for life.
2. When you're choosing flowers, remember that they wilt in heat and can be damaged by extreme

cold, too. Get recommendations from your florist about what kind will hold up best for the time of year and venue you've planned.

3. If you decide to do your own flowers, simpler is safer than complicated. Trust me, I know!

4. Bring a needle and thread because something *will* happen to the bridal gown! (One groom's mother saved the day by tacking up the bride's bustle, which detached accidentally on arriving at the reception hall.)

5. Remind your bridesmaids that if the matron of honor is pregnant and unable to bend over, they might need to adjust the bride's train and veil during the ceremony in her place.

When the Band Is a Bit Too Popular

Kellie Armstrong

WHEN MY HUSBAND, Jake, and I got married we wanted live music for our reception. All the DJs we'd seen in the past were awful and we wanted something different. Searching out and hiring a band was easy. We frequented a club on a regular basis, and one band that played there once in a while always packed the house. They were terrific, versatile, and we were impressed with their talent. There was no question in our minds that they were just right for our wedding.

We made arrangements to meet with them and booked them for the date. They were a bit pricey but we thought they were certainly worth the money. We never dreamed what was in store for us.

Arriving at the four-star hotel after the ceremony, we were escorted to the ballroom with the wedding party to be formally introduced as husband and wife. While waiting in the hall to make our grand entrance, we noticed two of the five band members making out with two girls on a couch directly in front of the ballroom entrance.

Soon the kissing turned to groping, and then one giggling girl was unbuttoning her shirt. In broad daylight, in view of my guests! Jake and the other guys in the wedding party thought it was hilarious, but I thought otherwise, and so did my bridesmaids.

My maid of honor went over to give them an earful, but stopped short when the ballroom doors opened and the other band members appeared to collect the two lost souls. They casually brushed the girls aside, proceeded into the ballroom, and two minutes later, still in shock, Jake and I were introduced into the ballroom.

As the reception went on, the two girls were caught twice trying to slip into the ballroom. Both times, the restaurateur firmly escorted them into the lounge. We later found out that the girls were groupies for the band and followed them everywhere. Everywhere but into my wedding reception, that is.

Later that day as I went into the lounge to smoke, I again had the pleasure of seeing these sleazy young ladies. As before, they each were wrapped around a male, only this time they were with two other band members, who conveniently happened to be taking their break in the bar.

The band played as well or even better than we expected. They had the whole place up and dancing, we got a lot of compliments from our guests, and even the restaurateur liked the music. But I sure could have done without the groupie show!

SURVIVAL HINTS

1. Be sure that the professionals you hire know you expect them to behave in a professional manner, and if you're hiring a popular band, make it clear that they are not allowed to bring guests or invite groupies or fans to your private event.

2. Even when hiring your first choice of musicians or DJs, sometimes the unexpected still happens. If you see something you don't like, be sure to say something, or ask someone you trust to handle it. After all, you're paying for a service and you are entitled to get what you paid for!

The Wedding Cake Catastrophe

Beth Wong

TWO YEARS BEFORE my wedding, I began subscribing to just about every major bridal magazine in print. I was in search of the perfect wedding gown and the even-more-perfect wedding cake. I had a picture in my mind of just what this cake would look like, but could not have explained my vision to a baker if my life depended on it. So I searched and searched until one day my page-turning fingers turned their very last page.

There it was—the cake of my dreams. Eight layers, creamy white, and decorated with beautiful pink roses that gradually grew smaller from the bottom to the top of the cake. A vine intertwined the roses and wound between the layers. It was the most gorgeous cake I had ever seen. *This* was my wedding cake, exactly as I'd dreamed it would look. I simply had to have it!

Picture in hand, I went from bakery to bakery, trying to find just the right one to create this confectionary masterpiece. It took weeks to find a bakery I trusted, and at last I had placed the order to make my wedding cake dreams come true. It was to be chocolate cake with raspberry filling, with whipped cream icing. Along the way, at each of the bakeries, I had also engaged in a taste-testing venture (and ended up putting on a few unnecessary extra pounds thanks to their tasty samples).

When the big day finally arrived I couldn't wait to see my gorgeous cake. I took a sneak peek through the reception door as we waited for the guests to be seated. Much to my amazement and horror, I spied the back of my wedding cake. The roses had been crushed and the vines were smeared. It was an eight-layered mess! When I got closer to take a look, I saw that the rest of the cake still seemed to be in perfect condition, but only from the front. I couldn't believe my eyes. What in heaven's name had happened to my pretty wedding cake?

Upset and confused, I was about to throw a fit when the DJ announced us and off we marched into the dining room. Almost literally having to hold my tongue, I controlled myself long enough to proceed into the room.

Moments later, the maître 'd asked to speak with me. A waiter had accidentally slipped when carrying a large tray of glasses and when he stood up, he lost his balance and landed partly on our cake.

Realizing that the baker wasn't at fault helped me calm down. The restaurateur offered to split the cost of the cake with us, since they'd damaged it, and because they'd moved the cake so it was now against the wall instead of in the center of the room, nobody else ever noticed the damage. And even though it was mashed on one side, that cake still tasted like heaven, and the flavor was further enhanced by that drastically reduced price!

SURVIVAL HINTS

1. When you're planning a major event like a wedding, things can sometimes go wrong. Rather than letting it spoil your day, try to ignore something that you can't change. There's so much else to be happy about, it's really not that important in the scheme of things.
2. Sometimes the only way to get through a trying moment is to get a grip on your tongue and relax.

Is That Seafood Newburg or Bait on My Buffet?

Danielle Fracas

MY IN-LAWS-TO-BE insisted we have our reception at this big Italian restaurant that the closest of their friends just happened to own. Not wanting to start out on the wrong foot with them I agreed. I knew my husband had dined there frequently and knew their best dishes. To assure me that everything would be fine he had taken me there to have dinner on a couple of different occasions. Every time the food proved to be superb. The service was great and the chef had actually come out of the kitchen to speak with us directly. I thought we were making the right decision and so I agreed: The reception would be held where his parents wanted.

The night before our wedding we held our rehearsal dinner at this same restaurant. All our guests were enjoying their meals when we began to hear screaming and yelling from the kitchen. Looking around nonchalantly we tried to keep the conversations going at the table to drown out the ruckus stirring in the background. And I think we did a good job of it until we heard the glass start shattering and the screaming intensify. Our table went silent as the chef came flying out of the kitchen, threw his hat on the floor, and told the owners, my in-laws' best friends, to shove their job and then stormed out the door.

I was in a state of panic. My wedding was the following day. He was not only *their* chef but mine. What was I going to do? The owners noticed the look of panic on my face and came over immediately to our table. They assured me that this was indeed typical behavior of Chef Kermit and he would be fine in a few short hours and back on the job. Dealing with Kermit's idiosyncrasies was well worth having a chef of his caliber in their kitchen. He was highly regarded in the area.

Feeling better about the situation, we finished up our dinner and left for the evening. With my fiancé and in-laws assuring me over and over that things tomorrow would run smoothly, I calmed down.

The big day came. The ceremony, the limos, the photographs, everything was right on time and as scheduled. It was perfect. When we arrived at the restaurant, the buffet table was gorgeous, set from end to end with fresh white and red roses. What was *not* gorgeous was the main dish. The Seafood Newburg that we had ordered, a creamy, cheese-laden seafood dish served over rice, did not at all look like the Seafood Newburg Kermit had made for us, but more like a sterling silver chaffing pan full of something offshore fisherman would use to attract sharks. Whatever it was, it definitely was not the Seafood Newburg I had tasted or ordered.

Turns out Kermit never came back after the blowup at the rehearsal dinner, and this dish had been prepared by the owners, who knew nothing about cooking. Believe it or not, it actually didn't taste bad—once we got past how it looked long enough to get it into our mouths!

SURVIVAL HINTS

1. Be prepared to tell your in-laws or anyone else who demands you do something you don't agree with that it's your wedding. While you'll make an effort to accommodate everyone, the final decisions are really up to you.

2. Trust your gut instincts if something doesn't feel quite right. Say something before it's too late to do anything about it.

A Place for Everyone

Marcy Vandertel

DO YOU HAVE relatives who don't get along? I suppose we all have them. It's not just you. Planning a major event such as a wedding can be fun but also very grueling. Any event mixing a large group of people who don't ordinarily spend time together is tricky. Some will get along while others won't. Some may be known rivals that you can count on to set sparks flying, while others will sit back timidly and watch as the fights brew. It's kind of like mixing water and oil—no matter how much you stir, it simply won't mix.

For this very reason I paid extra special attention to my wedding reception seating chart. I didn't want aunts who didn't get along or uncles who always fight to be seated together because I knew in the end it would only create havoc on my wedding day, a day that I wanted free of arguments.

My family sort of thrives on arguing. I think they actually enjoy it. There is always someone there to liven up the party with a jab or two, just to get that adrenaline going. My grandmother, now deceased, was a great one for this. She always knew just the right words to get all of them going. The funny thing is, though, she would start the argument then sit on the sidelines and watch as it escalated. It was especially funny because they never realized that it was Grandmother who had created the havoc.

As for the seating chart, in order to accommodate the large number of guests we had invited, the restaurateur suggested using the large round tables as they could accommodate two additional people compared to the rectangular ones. We agreed because in the end it would mean one less table and more open space.

The only problem with a round table is that even if your rivals aren't seated next to each other, they will be seated across from one another, and that may be worse yet. At least with a rectangular table you can seat Aunt Mary at one end and Aunt Ethel at the other, and although they can catch a glimpse of each other now and then, they are out of immediate danger of hostility. Although I ended up going with the round tables, I made sure everyone was seated with people known to be noncombative. And to assure myself that people sat where I intended, we used place cards at each seat. Every one of our guests thus had a specific assigned seat rather than just a particular table, and to make sure they remained in their assigned seats we asked the restaurateur to remove any unoccupied chairs when the reception began.

This solution worked like a charm for us. The reception went off without any signs of turmoil, and we were all the happier to have everyone included on our special day.

SURVIVAL HINTS

1. If you have antagonistic relatives or friends, try to carefully orchestrate where they are seated to avoid trouble.
2. If you have a large number of guests, consider putting bitter enemies at tables where they can't see—or hear—each other!

When Your Hotel Won't Cooperate, or When East Meets Midwest

Ken Hastie

HIS NAME WAS—and still is, actually—Ray Zardetto. A relatively simple name. Not too many consonants or syllables. No silent letters or anything like that. Pretty straightforward, or so one would think.

But do remember *that* name. Ray Zardetto.

It was about eighteen years ago. Our good friend, Ray, a lifelong New Jersey resident, and his fiancée, Rita, who hailed from the suburbs of the midwest Second City, Chicago, had arranged a June wedding in Chi-Town.

They had collectively and kindly invited their friends and family from all over the country to the shores of

Lake Michigan, where this particular weekend of that year, weather patterns were making such an unbelievable 100-plus-degree blast furnace of the locale that it made Hades seem like a shady spot.

In simple New Jersey-ese—where my other friend Sammy and I and our respective spouses hailed from—*It was friggin' hot!* I swear, when the four of us stepped out of O'Hare airport to head to the rental car pickup, we saw other weary fellow travelers burst into flames as they stepped outside of the airport proper with their luggage in tow. Such was the heat.

Imagine two Garden Staters in tuxedos reacting to this! Not to mention our lovely Jersey Girl legalized dates in their respective late 1980s East Coast gowns. Ray who? Let's get back on that damn plane!

Sucked it up, though, is what we did. Ray was our friend. Yes, Ray Zardetto. The man with that special, simple name. He was our longtime friend, and this was his and Rita's particularly special day. But damn! Dragging that luggage to the rental car and packing it in—with that kind of heat, *in tuxedos*—well, it was like dragging a body into a trunk! (OK. Insert your Jersey joke here. Go ahead. You're going to, anyway.)

Nevertheless, without undue hesitation—and because, as usual, we were running late—our melting little four-person NJ contingent sped our rental car to the church out in the Chicago suburbs. We arrived just in time to take our places as part of the wedding party, sweating profusely though we were. Everything, from a ceremonial hitching standpoint, was fine.

Now here was an additional good thing. There was this fairly sizeable multihour time gap between the actual nuptials and the reception. "Excellent," decided the four Jerseyites! We could go find the hotel that Ray had apparently reserved for us, check in, dump our luggage, splash some much needed cool water on ourselves, and if we got really lucky, find a place nearby that did one-hour Martinizing to revitalize our collectively sweat-sodden monkey suits. The funny thing is, none of us knew—and still don't—what Martinizing actually is. Nevertheless, we were all convinced that it takes one hour, no matter where you happen to be. We had the time. We felt encouraged.

Cut to next scene: The faux-marbled lobby of a hotel on the outskirts of the city where Mr. Zardetto had reserved a block of rooms for his traveling guests. Sans valet service for some reason, Bill and I had just dragged our luggage in the blistering noontime sun across a parking lot that seemed to cover acres and acres. In New Jersey, you could have fit a few towns and a few hundred residents into such a space. This was also, by the way, a time *before* they actually put wheels on luggage. Yes. There actually was such an uncivilized, backward time as recently as the late 1980s, and we found ourselves in it. Did I mention that we were in tuxedos and 100-plus-degree heat?

So, Bill and I were more than happy to get to that front desk to be greeted and checked in by our very cheerful customer representative, Jill. She was a hopelessly wholesome-looking farmer's-daughter type straight out of central casting, with a sweet smile and just the exactly correct freckle count. She was All-American perfect. We felt we were in excellent hands as we began our check-in dialogue.

"Good afternoon, gentleman. Welcome to the Rasinfratz. How may I help you?"

"How you doin'?" said I, with my most polite Jersey greeting. "We'd like to check in. We're here with the Ray Zardetto party. My friend here, his name is Coughlin, Bill Coughlin, and my name is Hastie, Ken Hastie. Again, we're both with the Ray Zardetto party."

"Okay. Let me see here . . ." A brief silence except for rapid typing on the keyboard and intent staring at the computer screen. "Hmmm. I'm very sorry sir, but I'm not showing any reservations for Coughlin or Hastie. And I'm not aware of any parties today for Razor Detto."

"Huh?? Are you sure? We're part of the Ray Zardetto party. It's a wedding group and they had booked several rooms here for the out-of-town guests—which we are, Mr. Coughlin and me, Mr. Hastie. This is the Rasinfratz Hotel on West Orchard, right?"

"Yes it is. And again, welcome to the Rasinfratz! Unfortunately though, we have no record of any reservations for Coughlin or Hastie. And again, I'm showing no Razor Detto party here either today."

"That Zardetto knucklehead!!" I say in an aside to Bill. "He must have forgotten to coordinate here with the front desk."

"Let's try this again. Jill—can I call you Jill?—Could you please check again for Ray Zardetto in your system there? To my knowledge, they are guests of the hotel here already. In fact, I'm pretty sure I saw their car in the lot as we came in. Perhaps we can raise them on the house phone and get them down here to confirm that we're part of their reservation block or add us if for some reason we were left off the list. How's that?"

"So sir, you'd like me to raise R. Detto? I really can't do that, I'm afraid. First of all, we don't have any R. Detto's listed, so I can't raise them on the house phone. And even if we did, I am not authorized to just raise the count of their reservation block without their permission. So, I'm very sorry Mr. Hastie, I just can't raise R. Detto. I'm sorry too that we are absolutely booked to capacity today."

At this point, Bill and I looked at each other in bewildered amazement. Either our farmer's-daughter friend Jill here had had a tragic farm equipment accident in her youth that somehow involved her head . . . or Allen Funt had risen from the dead and was hiding a camera somewhere in the lobby . . . or perhaps we were channeling Abbott and Costello in some kind of lost *Twilight Zone* episode! Desperate and nevertheless undaunted, we collectively tried again, this time asking Jill to bring in a supervisor of some sort for translation purposes. Jill complied.

"Jill, look. We're trying to locate a guest of your hotel to help us sort this out. His name is Ray Zardetto.

That's RAYMOND ZARDETTO. We call him Ray, for short. It's a fairly common shortening of the name, Raymond. Hell, he even calls himself by the name, Ray. And anyway—"

"See here, Mr. Hastie and Mr. Coughlin. There is no reason to use curse words with our staff here at the Rasinfratz!" broke in the supervisor. "I'm not going to stand here and let you speak to Jill that way. Look, she's explained to you. We have no record of reservations for either of you. We have no Razor Detto party scheduled here today. We have no guest by the name of R. Detto so we cannot raise them on the phone, nor can we raise the R. Detto room count on a reservation block we don't have. I suggest you find another hotel. There are others here on West Orchard. I suggest you try them."

Bill and I were speechless at this point . . . well, not completely. I decided on one last ditch effort, employing the pleading and sympathy approach.

"Look, we're really worn out here. It's 105 degrees outside by now. We're sweating up a storm in these tuxes, hauling luggage all over the place. Our wives, over there, are worn out too. We have to be at a wedding reception in just a little while and we'd love to freshen up before that. All we're trying to do is get ahold of Ray Zardetto. You know what I mean, don't you?"

"Okay, Mr. Hastie. We do have a nice public restroom around the corner. It's really very nice and very clean. We can watch your luggage for you. We have a beautiful gift shop right over there. It's filled with all kinds of toiletries and things. They may even have those Detto Razors or Razor Dettos you've been talking about, though I'm not sure. You could freshen up a little and . . . "

Arrrrgggg!!! Bill and I, at this point, could only walk away to a nearby lobby couch, totally stupefied and half hysterical with laughter. Our wives came over to see what was going on and asked if we could go to our rooms now.

We explained that we were not checked in at the Rasinfratz, nor apparently would we ever be. They looked at us incredulously. All I could muster was, "Go try and check in at that desk. Go ahead. We dare you." Looking at us very strangely and half perturbed, they took us up on our dare.

While the ladies were at the front desk, presumably getting lobotomized by Jill and team, I turned to Bill with a never-say-die idea. "You know Bill, maybe we *should* go to that gift shop and ask for Detto Razors or Razor Dettos. As back asswards as this place is, they just might check us into rooms, right at the gift shop cash register!"

Well, in ten minutes, our spouses returned, eyes spinning like pinwheels, muttering monosyllabic grunts. They too, were stupefied. We all sat down exasperated on the lobby couch, wondering what possible move we could try next.

Just then, the elevator doors slid open, and there, in their complete nuptial splendor, stepped out the brand spanking new Mr. and Mrs. Ray Zardetto!!

Bill and I quickly explained our dilemma as concisely as we could to our host—the man with the apparently troublesome name—and then watched as he went over to the front desk where he was greeted like a long-known Gold Card VIP and handed two room keys for us in a matter of seconds.

Well, apparently, Ray was known as just plain Mr. Zardetto at the Rasinfratz—the one permutation we didn't try in our approaches to this peculiar hotel front desk. Who knew? Who would think you would have to know?

Anyway, it all worked out well in the end, and the episode has provided much laughter over the years in its retelling.

Capturing the Memories

Cindy Matchett

THE PROBLEM WAS, I already had the images in my mind.

With each turn of the luxurious silky pages of *Martha Stewart* and *Elegant Boston Weddings*, I was forming my own picture-perfect memories months before our wedding day even took place: The charming snapshot of the seated couple from behind, holding hands under the table at the reception. The father's tender kiss giving his daughter away at the beginning of the ceremony. The close-up of the mother-in-law with tears in her eyes as the groom's brother offers the toast. And, the keeper, the photo we would enlarge to poster size and frame to hang above the fireplace: The bride and groom stumbling through a meadow, or along a beach, clinging to each other and laughing in sheer delight, such was their incredible joy at their love for each other.

These mental pictures were such a part of my wedding day, I could almost touch them. Never mind that we weren't getting married anywhere near a meadow or a beach, and we weren't planning on formal toasts. None of that had the power to alter the image of us sitting in our living room with our sage-green, fabric-covered scrapbook-style album—the latest trend, according to the magazines—and reminiscing fondly over the scenes, pleased that the photographer had captured us all so well.

My first exploratory phone call was to a photographer named Beatrice, whose ad, a black-and-white photo of a couple on a trolley car, I had carefully circled in my research.

"Hi!" I said brightly, "I'm getting married on August 16."

"Congratulations!" she said, as all the vendors do.

Enthusiastically, I continued, "I love your work, and was wondering if you are available, and also what your prices would be."

She paused, searching her calendar. "Luckily, I am available that day. My packages start around ten thousand dollars. Would you like to arrange an appointment to see some of my sample albums?"

I couldn't speak. Stunned, I stared down at the smiling bride leaning out of the trolley.

"How is this Thursday evening for you?"

Finally, I managed to stutter, "I think you are a bit out of our price range. Thank you so much anyway." I hung up the phone as if I had been slapped.

Time for Plan B: the Internet. I still didn't realize that the magazine photos I loved were often done in studios with strobes and models, or by very skilled, very exclusive, and expensive professionals. While I searched online for our affordable dream photographer, unaware of my naïveté, I drank in award-winning sepia-toned images of the couple's first dance, vivid groups of giggling bridesmaids in bright raspberry taffeta on kelly green lawns, and candid shots of wide-eyed children gazing out from chapel pews. These seemed like portrayals of real weddings for real people. I held fast to my vision, certain it was still attainable.

After exchanging a few e-mails, we arranged to meet the next photographers, Amelia and Derek, in their studio on a side street of one of New England's charming historical towns. There was a black-and-white poster of a smiling baby in one window, and a color poster of a bride staring thoughtfully at her bouquet in the other window. Inside, it was cool and inviting. Amelia ushered us to a chic purple couch and offered us a dish of wrapped chocolates. So far, so good. She introduced her husband, Derek, a meek slim man in his late twenties, and began to stack heavy leather albums into our laps. The images were fresh, relaxed, and observant.

"For that one, Derek used a fish-eye lens. He loves the fish-eye lens. Don't you, Derek?" Derek nodded with a shy smile at us as we flipped through the pages.

"Oh, *that* poor couple," Amelia continued, "they got poison ivy all over themselves the day before the wedding, trying to pick wildflowers for their reception. We had to stand them in the shade for all the formals so it wouldn't show. Can you imagine trying to pick your own flowers?"

I could, and had, in fact. I kept my gaze down and tried to focus on the hapless couple, feeling a sudden kinship with them. Amelia started again, this time pointing to a different pair. "Now *that* bride, my goodness, an older one, bless her heart—she didn't seem to care that much about her appearance. I mean, she wore her glasses all day! Derek did what he could with her."

I readjusted my own glasses, which I planned to wear at our wedding, and continued to turn pages. I was getting a headache.

"This is an amazing shot," I said to Derek, gesturing to a rolling lawn where the whole wedding party had been assembled.

"Derek worked hard for that shot, didn't you? I told him, 'You get up on that ladder and you don't come down until you get that shot,' didn't I?"

"I had a broken ankle," said Derek.

"And with a broken ankle too. I told him, too, 'Now don't you come down until you get the shot,' and he did.

It's a great shot." She looked at the book fondly. I glanced at my fiancé, Mike. He winked at me.

OK, so it's not only the photographer's art that I needed; the photographers themselves had to fit the fantasy. I didn't want Amelia risking Derek's life and limb at our wedding, thank you very much. Didn't seem like good karma.

So we moved on. Over the next two months, we met with nine photographers. The search took more time than any other part of our planning. I had hired the first caterer I met, without even tasting her food, because she had great references and I loved her personality. We chose the third site we visited, a horticultural center, because it was beautiful and had parking and would let us stay past midnight. We chose a blues band from a brochure we received; we went to hear them, loved them, and booked them the next day. All of these choices turned out to be fantastic. Why, then, was the photographer such a challenge?

Growing up, I *had* been one of those girls who dreamed wistfully of her wedding. By this point I was thirty-four years old and had been reading wedding magazines for nineteen years. I hadn't been dreaming of bands or food, or even locations. But I had been staring at the beautiful wedding scenes through all those geeky, ugly-duckling years of mine, fascinated by the confident brides, enthralled by the grooms who looked at them adoringly, cheered at how their families celebrated their choices and proudly toasted who they had become. Would I ever feel that way? Would I ever love or be loved with such joy? If I ever had a wedding, would I look like that in my own photos?

We found Monica almost by accident. I was preparing for a two-week business trip, and, discouraged, had put the photographer project on hold. A few days before I left, I went to the library to do some preparatory research. On a break, I slid into a padded chair at one of the library computers and logged onto one of my favorite wedding planning Web sites. Halfheartedly, out of habit, I clicked through the local photographer listings, and sat up suddenly. There was one I hadn't seen before. Monica's Web site was friendly, easy to read, and had lovely images. With a handful of change, I punched her number into the payphone by the ladies' room. She thought it was amusing that I was old-school enough to use a payphone, which made me laugh, and agreed to come to our house the following evening. She was polite, organized, and very down-to-earth. Her albums, collections of her best work, were elegant and told all the beautiful stories I was looking for. She said she did a mix of portraits and photojournalism, would bring an assistant, and would help us put together a creative artsy album. The next morning, we signed the contract and Mike mailed it on the way back from taking me to the airport. We had done it!

On the day of the wedding, I first noticed something was wrong when my best friend knelt to pin her family's blue handkerchief to my petticoat, and Monica simply stood by the bookcases watching.

Surprised, I said to her, "I'd love a shot of this, if we could."

That was a recognizable wedding moment, wasn't it? I had warned her I didn't want any "getting dressed" shots, none of the awkward views so popular with all the photographers of me in my undergarments maneuvering into the dress. Perhaps she thought the petticoat counted as one of those. I tried to relax.

I forgot about Monica completely as I walked up the garden path with my dad while our minister played her guitar, listened to our friends read our favorite poems, told Mike I chose him as my husband, and kissed him when he chose me as his wife. The gathering of family and friends felt warm and magical, and I had never been so happy. A heron flew across the pond behind us during the ceremony, Mike's eyes filled with tears as the music started, his nephew snuck a huge fingerful of cake icing during the reception, and our guests all joined us on the dance floor for a surprise polka. Mike and I were both so filled with gratitude and pride that our loving friends and family were there to celebrate with us, and amazed that we had found each other. The day flew by, and from time to time, I thought of the photos Monica was taking, relieved to know we could come back to these wonderful moments later and savor them as we looked at the album. But it was not to be.

When Monica's assistant fainted twice during the ceremony from not eating breakfast, I didn't notice, though everyone else did. Only afterward I heard that she cornered some of our guests and ranted to them about her assistant, and that the site coordinator thought Monica was "awful." But it wasn't until the proofs came that I cried.

The squares of photo paper spread out before us felt cold and lifeless; all the moments I was looking for just weren't there. There was nothing to say or do. Though he was disappointed too, Mike encouraged us to order the album anyway. Most of the time, it sits in its box in our dining room closet. Years later, I have come to see that the photos Monica took at our wedding weren't terrible. I have heard worse stories. They were different from my own mental images. As an artist myself, I understand now that these were her own subjective interpretation of the event, and yes, she was having a bad day.

I do have a favorite photo from the wedding, snapped by a friend while Mike and I kissed under a tree just after the ceremony. It sits in a small frame on our coffee table, and every time I look at it, all the loving feelings of the day come flooding back. The professional photography I had yearned for, mirroring back to me the adult I had hoped to magically become, transformed like a fairy tale that day, did not occur. But I've learned that this kind of change has to come from within. And while I work on that, I have a lifetime of memories to create with Mike—real memories, for better or for worse, to have and to hold, for as long as we both shall live.

SURVIVAL HINTS

1. Keep your focus on what matters—honoring and celebrating your loving relationship with each other, and sharing it with your supportive community.

2. Don't try to control the things you can't; remember to slow down and really take in what is happening that day. If your photographer turns out to be less than you expected, you will always have your own special memories.

8

When It's Your Second Time Around

Sanity Quiz

You're getting married and you've decided to include your extended family in the wedding party, which includes your stepsister's two young children. Your stepniece Stacy will be fine; she's nine and you think she can handle it with ease. But her little brother Bobby is only five, so one day he wants in and the next he wants out. He just can't seem to make up his mind! Your stepsister is thrilled that you've included her whole family, but Bobby's waffling is really making you nervous.

Do you:

A. tell your stepsister she needs to help Bobby make up his mind

B. talk to Bobby yourself and see if you can get him to promise to cooperate

C. tell your stepsister you're sorry, but you don't think it's going to work out and that Bobby is out of the wedding

D. take your chances on a five-year-old whose only full-time commitment so far has been to watch cartoons

If you answered yes to any one of these questions, then you've got kids in your wedding. Read on and see how our contributors coped!

Swept Away

Patty Swyden Sullivan

HOW DID I, a mature divorced woman, plan my wedding to the man of my dreams? With all the confidence of a two-ton hippo tiptoeing on the eggshells of diplomacy. I planned this middle-aged, second-time-around wedding under my self-imposed limitations that people our age should quietly go away, do the deed, and return with as little disruption to life as possible—the de-secret-izing factor falling somewhere between an American Indian woman leaving the tribe to give birth in the wilderness and a Viking funeral sans death and fire.

Also weighing on my self-conscious approach to our nuptials were the feelings of our adult children. My fiancé's three children struggled with the loss of their mother. My two children were still battling the disappointment of their parents' "perfect" marriage becoming derailed by divorce. All had a reasonable right to be wary of this new union, regardless of the guarded but encouraging smiles they put forth.

But I also had to consider the reaction of family and friends who received the news of our engagement with an almost embarrassing degree of exuberance. They pumped my fiancé's hand up and down, slapped him on the back, and grinned at him like mad hatters. The words, "Hallelujah, we are off the hook," resonated on their beaming faces. If their relief had been any greater, the wind from their collective sigh would have leveled nearby trailer parks.

In defense of their enthusiasm, my dear friends and family had nurtured me after my unexpected divorce left me disillusioned and emotionally catatonic. They tended my wounds and helped me heal. Now the miracle of a new love, unbridled happiness, and my very own Prince Charming were at hand. My friends wanted to celebrate! They started planning an event befitting a coronation. I reproached them, saying the upcoming nuptials required a bit more decorum. After all, any blushing on my part was not due to me being demure, but instead to the rising heat from my hot flashes.

I tried to explain that I did not want to appear greedy for life's rewards. It was nothing short of miraculous that I had found my other half, the part of me I did not even realize I had been missing, but who now was integrated into my soul. Dare I continue the clichés? Yes. This man completed me. Eager to start our lives together, I did not need all the frills: I only needed Bob.

Torn between my awkwardness at displaying too much attention to the nuptials out of respect for our children, our age, and for second marriages, and not wanting to offend those who wanted to be a part of this occasion, I became a two-headed master attempting to meet the concerns of everyone, thus risking satisfying no one. Bob and I would not elope to take our vows in secret, but neither would we fall prey to an overblown party.

As the weeks drew nearer to our selected date, enthusiastic supporters applied more pressure. Where will the reception be? Have you picked out your dress? You need to book a photographer and florist early. Hop, hop. Even I realized that certain tasks must be accomplished. But I was determined to fulfill only necessary needs and keep this wedding simple, routine, and underwhelming.

We reserved the church, stressing to the church wedding coordinator (when did they create that job?) the small size of the guest list. I feared that the enormous number of pews would devour them. Jokingly, the coordinator pointed out that the number of choir seats exactly matched the number of our guests. Her smile faded when I told her to ask the priest for his permission to use them.

Next, I flipped through my closet to see if I had something appropriate to wear. Not finding a dress that conveyed I-may-*be*-the-bride-but-I-don't-want-to-*look*-like-the-bride, I headed for the mall. I pulled a chocolate brown dress off the rack. Its color combined with an

elongated bodice and flowing skirt were the perfect cam-
ouflage not only for the occasion, but also for my hips.

Rapidly crossing off must-do items, I visited the owner
of a neighborhood floral shop. She proudly displayed
elaborate arrangements for the church. I pooh-poohed
her enthusiasm with a dismissive wave of my hand. Not
one to be pooh-poohed lightly, she steered me to non-
flowering plants that could be donated to the church
after the ceremony. Then with the ease of a skilled thera-
pist, she interspersed questions about my engagement
with the gathering of billing information. By the time I
left, she knew more about my intimate relationships than
my hairdresser.

Another quick stop and I hired a photographer to
snap a few family photos before the ceremony. After all,
we needed something for the mantle. Finally, I arranged
for a light dinner to follow the service. Our party would
not quite fill a small private dining room at a nearby
country club. We would dine on glazed chicken, rice,
and grilled vegetables. One could not protest too much
festivity over being fed such straightforward food.

The proverbial big day arrived. I was prepared for a
straightforward run-through of the events as I had
planned them. No fuss, no muss. We say the vows, we eat
some chicken, everyone goes home, and Bob and I are
off to the Caribbean for ten days of enchantment.

When Bob and I arrived at the church, we found our
family gathered in the social room. The photographer
had set up her equipment for the posed photographs.

Systematically, she took group shots of our children, parents, and siblings. She concluded with formal poses of the bride and groom.

Just as we finished, the chatty florist bubbled through the church door. She had placed potted palms at the altar earlier in the day. Now she came running in carrying a white florist box.

"I know you nixed a bridal bouquet. Think of this as a fashion statement."

She gently placed in my hands seven individual tulips bound together by one delicate satin ribbon. "There is a flower for each member of your new family." I marveled at how their simple beauty enhanced my gown. Suddenly I saw how this marriage would adorn all our lives—Bob and I would see to that—just as these flowers graced my gown. I looked up to Bob to see if he noticed; his smile told me he did.

Bob took my arm and we strolled up to the candlelit altar. Our loved ones encircled us in their choir seats. Nestled in their warmth, we felt serenity settle over us. As the priest began the service, he started to tell our stories. Of course, everyone present knew the intimate details of our histories. But listening to the priest describe the loss of a life partner, crises of faith, faith renewed, and the miracle of second chances eliminated all the pretense that our age and circumstances had put us beyond the reach of ritual. How could it have remained? The abundance of joy in my heart left no room for doubts about celebrating this marriage.

Recognizing joy is glorious, even in times when it evolves from sorrow. Trying to deny it is not only dishonest, but prevents planting the seed for the future. Bob and I wanted our life with our children to bloom to its full potential. At that moment, we let go of restraints and let loose the power of love for all to see.

The priest pronounced us married. Jubilantly, we strode down the aisle where the persistent photographer waited. Taking her cue from the florist, she had ignored my wishes for no candid photographs.

Bob, seeing her there, gave her a conspiratorial wink. The next thing I knew my feet were flying off the ground. My husband had lifted me up and swung me across his body, cradling me in his arms. The photographer clicked the shutter as Bob carried me across the threshold of our marriage, life, and family with the boldness of a man shouting to the world, "This is my wife!"

SURVIVAL HINTS

1. Even if you want a low-key wedding, it's still something to celebrate. Don't be afraid to go for it.
2. Small weddings can be wonderful because of the intimacy and because you have more time with the select few you've included, so don't be talked out of it if it's what you want.

A Little Wedding for a Big Marriage

Ginny Chandoha

MY HUSBAND AND I had both made brief marriage "mistakes" by the time we met. In fact, I was so leery of marriage that he had to repeatedly ask me to marry him for three years before I would say yes. Since we had both been through the big wedding with the wrong people, we decided that this time around it would be simple. And inexpensive.

At the time, we lived together in an apartment in a borough of New York City. Since we had lived together for three years, and were both divorced, I felt it would be ridiculous to wear a wedding gown and instead chose a fancy dress I thought I could wear for other occasions. It had a fitted, velvet bodice that laced up the front, and a long, lacy skirt with its own sliplike backing. I thought it was lovely at the time, but in retrospect, I think I looked more like a Swiss miss from a Riccola commercial.

Having been a flower child of the 1970s, I also didn't want a wedding ring. I didn't need some band of gold to prove that I was married. My prospective groom decided to wear slacks, plain shirt, jacket, and tie. We booked time at City Hall in New York City, where we would be married by a justice of the peace. The only other witness to this event would be my parents, my brother and sister-in-law, their two young children, and my husband's aunt. After the ceremony we would take everyone out to dinner nearby.

The wedding day arrived. We got ourselves gussied up, and took the subway from the Bronx to lower Manhattan, where we were to meet our family members. I remember people staring at us as we boarded the subway platform. At first I thought it was because we were all dressed up like we were going to a party on a weekday afternoon, but I soon discovered, to my horror, that in the light the skirt of my dress became see-through. I huddled as close to my future husband as possible, and then ran for a seat on the train.

Getting married at City Hall is not romantic at all. All of the marriage candidates sit in a large waiting room while some civil servant calls out the names, one by one, and the couples go into the nearby officiating room like sheep going to slaughter.

Finally our names were called, and we were led into the next room. We stood on a threadbare carpet in front of a very used wooden lectern with the initials of previous hopefuls carved into it. The official read through the non-religious script in a monotone. He came to the point where the wedding rings are exchanged, and he seemed totally flabbergasted when we said there were no rings. He stuttered and then whispered, "Oh, okay, I understand," like it was some big secret. In what seemed like five minutes or less, we were pronounced husband and wife.

The restaurant was only blocks away, and we all walked there together. It was before New York City had passed its pet cleanup rules, and my niece stepped in dog poop. She was extremely upset by this until my mother told her it was a sign of luck, which appeased her somewhat. Of course, my niece was too young to know that there is good luck, and bad luck, and stepping in dog doo wasn't necessarily a positive experience!

When we got to the restaurant, everyone ordered the meal of their choice. My nephew was unhappy with his dinner, and my husband graciously swapped dinners with him. It was a totally relaxed atmosphere as my family loved my husband, and I considered his aunt to be my surrogate mother. We kissed them all good-bye, hopped back onto the subway, and returned to our apartment as a married couple.

I have often thought of renewing our vows, having the wedding and reception we never had, with all of our friends and family in attendance. We have been together for thirty-four years now. Perhaps on our thirty-fifth or fortieth wedding anniversaries. But why ruin a good thing?

SURVIVAL HINTS

1. When you're planning a second wedding, it's up to you to decide what traditions you want to embrace or ignore.
2. Sometimes it takes a second try to get it right!

My Stepdaughter's Smile

B. R. Scotch

WHAT HAPPENS WHEN your five-year-old soon-to-be stepdaughter's front teeth fall out the day of your wedding? What do you do if you think the kid will freak at the mere mention of the word *dentist?* I kept trying to put myself into the girl's place. What exactly goes through your mind when you're a little kid with wiggly teeth, you're in your first wedding—and it happens to be your dad's?

When I was five, my cousin and his fiancée asked me to be the flower girl in their wedding. I was nearly beside myself with excitement over wearing a long dress like the rest of the bridesmaids, and it had been the thrill of my five-year lifetime. But now it was time for my own wedding, and it was going to be a lavish affair. It was important to make my stepdaughter, Sandra, feel important—after all, it was her dad's wedding and she was a precious part of it, too. It also gave me a chance to bond with her, as well as to reassure her that she had a place of honor, both at the wedding and in our future family.

So with the little one and my eleven bridesmaids, we went to a local bridal shop brimming with a vast array of selections for the wedding party. I had decided that all the bridesmaids would each wear a different colored pastel dress, and naturally this meant we had to find not only a dress that fit everyone, but also one that looked good on all of them. Luckily this bridal shop had several on-site seamstresses, so this meant that if necessary, they could make any of the full array of colors from scratch if they weren't manufactured in the shades required.

This colorful plan was indeed astonishing to my soon-to-be stepchild's eyes: She'd never even been to a wedding, never mind a rainbow wedding. Just about every pastel color would be represented—pink, baby blue, yellow, mint green, salmon, deep blue, lavender, and every shade in between. The little one was enthralled by the off-shoulder bridesmaids' gowns, each with three layers of tulle and a matching headdress. I made sure that she'd feel special by matching her dress to the same shade of blue as the maid of honor's gown, and she was thrilled.

We went back and forth for fittings, with Sandra always in tow. I didn't want her to think we'd ever leave her out, so we scheduled all the fittings around her school and dance class schedules—even though the bridesmaids had to scramble. Although she was small, she was growing, so we left her hem until the very last fitting, just days before the event—in case of a sudden growth spurt. Her little satin shoes were dyed to match, and she too would wear long white gloves, just like the grown-up bridesmaids.

Soon the day approached. Sandra's hair was cut and styled, and she was instructed by her dad and me to smile as she walked down the aisle. But then came the crisis: One week before the wedding, my almost-stepdaughter's two front teeth became quite loose. Hardly good timing, but not a tragedy either. I was unconcerned.

Meanwhile, she showed everyone at the bridal shower: "Look, my teeth are wiggling!" My future mother-in-law's eyes widened at her granddaughter's plight, but my aunt reassured her: "They won't fall out yet, honey—don't worry!" Everyone nodded and smiled except for her wise grandmother, who whispered to me that she had a bad feeling about those teeth.

The day of the wedding arrived. As she chomped on her breakfast cereal, dining with her dad, Sandra felt a strange sensation. What was it? Oh no! Out fell those wiggly front teeth! Here was her big day, and now she'd be grinning with a gap—right in the middle of her smile. Ordinarily this was a pretty calm child, and nobody expected what came next—except her grandmom, of course. Instead of shrugging it off, the little girl threw a fit. She stomped out of the room, sulking, pouting, and crying. Then she announced she wasn't going to the wedding!

I'd have thought she'd be far too excited about her dress and the upcoming spectacle to worry about something like this. After all, she'd lost other teeth before. But her dad and grandmother pried out of her that she was nervous, confused about everything, and wished that her mom, who had died when the little girl was just three, could see her all dressed up. Not only that, but she was suddenly worried about walking down the aisle first—something she hadn't mentioned the night before at the rehearsal, but which she must have worried about the whole night.

Being a single parent for several years, my fiancé knew how to handle his daughter. He explained that she didn't have to worry about walking first down the aisle because if she didn't want to, she could walk with the first of the bridesmaids, or else she could walk with the ring bearer, who she liked. She nodded silently and agreed.

"And as for your mommy, she's up in Heaven and she will be watching everything today. I'm sure she's very proud of how her little girl is growing up, and she'll be with you the whole time." After a big hug and some kisses, she smiled and said, "Okay, Daddy."

At the church, the little one tried hard to keep her mouth closed, but when she saw me stepping from the limo in my dazzling wedding finery, her grin was so huge that I knew in an instant her front teeth were gone. With a big smile, I opened my eyes wide and pointed to my own front teeth and she began to giggle with delight that I'd noticed.

Inside the church, it was hard not to shed a tear as she marched down the aisle, head held high like a little soldier, with the ring bearer by her side. She looked like a little angel.

At the end of the day, my little stepdaughter had been the hit of the entire affair. As we were saying good-bye, she whispered in my ear that she was glad I would be her new mommy. It was indeed a very precious moment.

SURVIVAL HINTS

1. If you decide to include a small child in your wedding party, you'll need extra patience in explaining what you want them to do.
2. Remember that stepchildren often have unresolved feelings about their parent's divorce or death, so be extra vigilant in making sure they know they're an important part of the upcoming event and the new family that is being created.
3. Always try to put yourself in the stepchild's place when making wedding arrangements so that they feel included and special. It can make all the difference in how you relate in your future life together.
4. Make sure you exhibit maximum tact and patience when small stepchildren are involved, because there are always surprises!

The Preteen Witch in the Wedding

Cinnamon Capsico

I WAS REMARRYING, and to be diplomatic, I had to include Lucy, my least favorite preteen, in my wedding. Since I had no kids of my own, it seemed like a good idea to include her. She was my fiancé's stepniece—his brother's stepdaughter—and a rather surly, often obnoxious kid. But I did the right thing and asked her to be a junior bridesmaid. I knew I'd have to deal with Lucy at all future family events, and I might as well start off trying to make friends. Naively, I thought she'd be excited about being asked, and about getting a pretty new dress and her first high-heel shoes. Think again.

I took the bridesmaids on our first trip to the bridal shop, where they were all measured from head to toe. The girl was sullen and would barely cooperate. We had to go back a few times to be fitted, and each time it was an ordeal to have her around. She whined all the time and complained about everything. She hated the dress, she hated the color, she hated the shoes, and she hated the hat. What on earth do you do with a ten-year-old like that?

At the bridal shower, she sulked and even had a tantrum because she wanted to leave before all the gifts were opened so she could go see her friends. I truly hoped this kid would outgrow her bad behavior, because I wasn't looking forward to another ten years of this nonsense at every future family occasion until she eventually grew up.

We had the wedding rehearsal at the church, with the Franciscan priest in his brown robe, white rope belt, and sandals. He was delightfully funny and made us all laugh, and he made sure we knew what to do. But Lucy made some snotty remark, and finally my fiancé took her aside to set her straight, probably in fear that I was about to commit murder right on the spot.

At the rehearsal dinner I gave each bridesmaid a present—a beautiful necklace to wear with their dresses. Par for the course, my stepniece made a face and threw it on the table with her nose in the air. "I only wear white gold," she sniffed. I couldn't help but think that this kid really needed a muzzle and leash, and I'd be happy to provide them in white gold!

Finally the big day arrived. It was the end of May, and it coincidentally was Lucy's birthday—she was all of eleven years old, and was no doubt annoyed not to be the center of attention. She truly was a spoiled brat in every sense of the word.

Despite being given a beautiful watch by her mother and stepfather, along with the huge array of gifts she expected and demanded, she had actually complained to my fiancé that our wedding was keeping her from having her birthday party with her friends, and that they'd had to postpone that event at the skating rink. He raised an eyebrow and told her that her birthday wasn't going to be the focus of our attention today, but we still hoped she'd enjoy it. If not, she might rather stay home! She looked a little taken aback, but for a change didn't say a word.

The ceremony was beautiful and perfect, and Lucy actually cooperated, even though she slumped down the aisle. What could I do? I decided not to watch. The reception was at a large local banquet hall, the swankiest around. The room was large and decorated with murals, and the bridal party was seated at a long table high up in a balcony, looking down on the tables of guests below. Little did we know that this setting quite literally would be that junior witch-in-training's downfall.

The bridal party entered the balcony from a side door, and we all stood at the table overlooking the guests at their tables below. Soon the bandleader introduced the participants. The bridal party came down the steps in pairs, then posed on either side of the staircase. When Lucy descended the stairs, wearing the most hideous platform shoes ever built, and ones that didn't match her dress (despite being given a dyed pair), her shoe buckle caught on the hem of her dress, tangling her in it and tripping her. Down she lurched—on her way head-first toward the bottom of the steep long flight! Everyone gasped.

At the last possible second, just before she hit the floor, her stepfather—the best man—who'd already descended the stairs, grabbed her and stood her back on her platformed feet. She was gasping in fright and flailing her arms, then began to silently cry, streaming mascara down her now flushed cheeks. Her stepfather comforted her and she soon calmed down, even managing a giggle before very long. Catastrophe averted, we began to relax as we marched carefully down to the dance floor—all to thunderous applause.

We dined sumptuously and danced. Eventually the wedding cake was cut and everyone crowded around. To the drum roll we sliced, kissed, and ate, and then came the final surprise.

The bandleader announced a birthday and—to Lucy's great surprise—they wheeled out another cake—for her! To her shock and amazement, the entire roomful of guests sang "Happy Birthday," and we all ate two kinds of cake.

And to our delight, at the end of the evening, Lucy came over to me and whispered in my ear, "Thank you. I'm sorry I've been such a shrew." And thankfully, since that day she's always been happy to see me, and actually is becoming a sweet young lady. But whenever I think of her near catastrophe and transformation at my wedding, I still shake my head and smile.

SURVIVAL HINTS

1. If your wedding day is also a kid's birthday, especially a stepchild, be sure to remember the occasion and make a fuss over them. It can do a lot to heal old wounds and forge new bonds.
2. Whenever you're including kids in your wedding, remember that it's a big day for them and that they sometimes get overwhelmed.
3. Be extra careful on stairs—long dresses and high heels can be a treacherous combination!

Acknowledgments

The authors would like to acknowledge our contributors for making this book possible. In particular, we'd like to thank Ronda Kaysen, Patty Swyden Sullivan, Ken Hastie, Ginny Chandoha, Barbara A. Craig, and Arline Simpson, all of whom are repeat contributors to the Staying Sane series.

We'd also like to single out Wendy Holt, editor at Da Capo Press, for a special thank you: Your gentle and careful edits, helpful ideas, and great suggestions have made this a much better book!